The Catholic Biblical Quarterly
Monograph Series
28

The Use of Arabic in Biblical Hebrew Lexicography

BY

John Kaltner

The Catholic Biblical Quarterly
Monograph Series
28

Produced in the United States of America

Library of Congress Cataloging-in-Publication Data

Kaltner, John, 1954–
The use of Arabic in biblical Hebrew lexicography / by John Kaltner.
p. cm. – (Catholic biblical quarterly. Monograph series : 28)
Includes bibliographical references and index.
ISBN 0-915170-27-2 (alk. paper)
1. Hebrew language–Lexicography. 2. Hebrew language–Lexicology. 3. Hebrew language–Etymology. 4. Hebrew language–Foreign elements–Arabic. 5. Bible. O.T.–Language, style. I. Title. II. Series.
PJ4823.K35 1996
492.4'7–dc20
95-45182
CIP

Contents

Acknowledgments

It was through my association with the Catholic Foreign Mission Society of America (Maryknoll) that I first encountered the peoples and cultures of the Arabic-speaking world. That experience began a fascination with and interest in the Arabic language that continues to this day. I owe the Maryknoll Society, particularly the members of the Middle East Unit, an enormous debt of gratitude for the opportunity they provided me and the support they gave to me.

Professor Herbert Huffmon of Drew University gave much valuable advice and input in the course of my research and writing. With his assistance the idea for this project was first conceived and with his encouragement it reached completion. Professor George Krotkoff of Johns Hopkins University also offered many helpful comments and suggestions on Arabic lexicography and related matters. Both of them have my deepest thanks and appreciation. A final expression of gratitude goes to Debra Bartelli for her companionship, support and love. This work is affectionately dedicated to her.

CHAPTER 1

The Problem and the Resources

One of the most common ways biblical scholars attempt to uncover the sense of problematic Hebrew words whose meanings are unknown, or to propose new meanings for words which are well attested, is through appeal to cognate languages. A similar form in a related language whose meaning is clearly established, so the logic goes, can serve as an indicator that this same sense may be present for the Hebrew word as well. This type of approach to solving textual problems in the Hebrew bible has been used ever since the similarities between Hebrew and other Semitic languages were first recognized.[1]

Among the languages used for such purposes perhaps none has been more frequently cited than Arabic. In recent times other languages, especially Ugaritic and Akkadian, have been used much more commonly, but prior to the discovery and decipherment of these languages it was to Arabic that all biblical scholars engaged in comparative work first turned. This has resulted in an enormous body of literature which has accumulated over the years, in the form of both full-length articles and short notes at the end of scholarly journals, attesting to the significant role Arabic has played in research related to biblical Hebrew lexicography.[2]

[1] For a good overview of many of the issues related to this area of biblical scholarship see James Barr, *Comparative Philology and the Text of the Old Testament* (Winona Lake, IN: Eisenbrauns, 1987). This work, originally published in 1968, contains some helpful basic information on the complex question of the role of Arabic in comparative Semitics.

[2] Arabic remains the most extensive and richest corpus for comparative Semitic lexicography. Its imposing role is seen when one examines the index of examples found at the end of Barr's

This study will attempt to examine certain aspects of the use of Arabic in biblical Hebrew lexicography. In particular, it will focus upon the faulty methodology that is commonly employed by Hebraists in drawing upon the Arabic sources and it will identify a number of methodological problems which raise important questions about how best to make use of the enormously valuable body of data contained in the Arabic dictionaries. It should be acknowledged at the outset that, in most cases, biblical scholars have been careful in their use of the Arabic sources and correct in their interpretation of the evidence. However, in a significant number of cases their work has been less than satisfactory. This inadequate methodology appears even in the work of well-known scholars.[3] As a consequence of so many poor models, the traps for the unwary are ever at hand. This present work is intended to lessen the dangers.

Before turning to examples of such misuse, our topic must be placed in its proper context. The remainder of this chapter will briefly discuss three aspects of this context which will move from the general to the specific. The first section will treat some of the major figures and works of modern comparative Semitic study. The importance of developments in the area of general linguistics will be highlighted here as well as the central role of Arabic in the field. A second part of the context to be considered will be medieval Jewish scholarship. Here, too, significant individuals and works will be mentioned as will the primary influence Arabic exerted on the earliest Hebrew grammarians and lexicographers. We will conclude our study of the context with a discussion of Arabic lexicography. This must, of necessity, be a selective overview of scholars and works, but each of the six Arabic dictionaries that will figure prominently in later chapters will be described in some detail.

Modern Comparative Semitic Study

The first truly comprehensive work in comparative Semitics was that of E. Renan in 1855.[4] Only the first volume of this work was published, but it was an important first step in the field. It was soon overshadowed by the magnifi-

work (320–37). Of the 334 examples which he lists of proposals put forth by scholars, 167, exactly one-half, list Arabic as the language of comparison.

[3] Studies which are critical of biblical scholarship's use of Arabic are rare. A recent excellent example can be found in W. Johnstone's "*YDʿ* II, 'Be Humbled, Humiliated'?" *VT* 41 (1991) 49–62. This article will be discussed in more detail in Appendix A.

[4] E. Renan, *Histoire Génerale et Système Comparé des Langues Sémitiques I* (Paris: Michel Lévy Frères, 1855).

cent work of T. Nöldeke in 1887,[5] which is still of great value. Other significant contributions of last century include those of W. Wright and O. E. Zimmern.[6]

All of these early works helped to lay a solid foundation for the discipline and prepared the way for the contributions made by C. Brockelmann, who must be considered the grand master of comparative Semitists. His work initiated a new phase in the field, and his two-volume *Grundriß der vergleichenden Grammatik der semitischen Sprachen*, published between 1908 and 1913, remains the standard reference tool for all who engage in comparative Semitic work.

At about this time, fundamental changes were taking place within the study of linguistics. The typical way to study language prior to this was in a diachronic fashion under the aspect of historical comparison. There now emerged a synchronic and descriptive method which attempted analysis at one or several points along the line of a language's historical development. One result of this innovation was that the comparative historical approach which Semitists had been using was no longer the sole or dominant method within linguistic study, but became only a small part of what F. de Saussure, the founder of the discipline, termed "General Linguistics."[7]

This development had a profound impact on comparative Semitics. Scholars now began to take this new approach to linguistic study into account in their efforts.

An important work of the 1920's was that of G. Bergsträßer.[8] He tried to analyze and organize the Semitic languages by type, and this approach represented a step forward. Another significant advance was made by M. Cohen, who, for the first time, drew the Hamitic languages into the discussion in a careful and systematic way.[9] The most recent comprehensive work done in comparative Semitics, that of S. Moscati, et al.,[10] may be considered one of the

[5] T. Nöldeke, *Die semitischen Sprachen. Eine Skizze* (Leipzig: T. O. Weigel, 1887).

[6] W. Wright, *Lectures on the Comparative Grammar of the Semitic Languages* (Cambridge: University Press, 1890); H. Zimmern, *Vergleichende Grammatik der semitischen Sprachen* (Berlin: Reuther & Reichard, 1898).

[7] His ideas and method are found in his seminal work *Cours de Linguistique Générale* (Paris: Payot, 1916).

[8] G. Bergsträßer, *Einführung in die semitischen Sprachen* (München: M. Hueber, 1928). English translation, *Introduction to the Semitic Languages* (Winona Lake, IN: Eisenbrauns, 1983).

[9] M. Cohen, "Langues Chamito-Sémitiques," in *Les Langues du Monde* (ed. A. Meillet and M. Cohen; Paris: Centre National de la Recherche Scientifique, 1952) 81–181.

[10] S. Moscati, A. Spitaler, E. Ullendorff, W. von Soden, *An Introduction to the Comparative Grammar of the Semitic Languages* (Wiesbaden: Harrassowitz, 1964).

clearest examples of an effort which is informed by this new perspective. This shift in linguistic method early this century from a predominantly historical, diachronic approach to one that is also descriptive and synchronic offered a new perspective from which to engage in comparative study. Many scholars made ready use of these advances in linguistics. The application of these features to comparative Semitic study has often led to fresh and creative contributions.

Another key factor, often unmentioned, which has played a major role in the development of comparative Semitics is its origin as a tool for use in the study of biblical Hebrew. In its earliest stages, comparative Semitic study was primarily an attempt to analyze and explicate the biblical material. D. Cohen explains: "From this point of view, I believe that one can characterize Semitic lexicography, in its comparative and etymological aspects, by an essential trait: its exegetical origin which marked the entire course of its development."[11] This point is critical because, as Cohen observes, to a large extent this originating context shaped the future direction of comparative Semitics.

The status of Hebrew as a sacred language led earlier scholars in the West to base their work on the mistaken principle that Hebrew was the "original" member of the Semitic language family.[12] Such ideas continued to circulate until the nineteenth century, but perhaps no scholar took the notion to the extreme that Estienne Guichard did, as evidenced by the title of his 1613 dictionary: *L'harmonie étymologique des langues hébraïque, chaldaïque, syriaque, grecque, latine, française, italienne, espagnole, allemande, flamande, anglaise, etc., en laquelle, par plusieurs antiquités et étymologies de toute sorte, se démontre évidemment que toutes les langues sont descendues de l'hébreu*.

A situation developed, then, in which Hebrew was viewed as the parent tongue and Arabic and the other Semitic languages were seen as its offspring, with Aramaic as a corrupted form of Hebrew. This situation changed rather

[11] D. Cohen, "La Lexicographie Comparée," *Quaderni di Semitistica* 2 (1973) 191. S. Segert, in "Hebrew Bible and Semitic Comparative Lexicography," *VTSup* 17 (1968) also notes the exegetical origin of comparative Semitics and raises the important point that extant comparative dictionaries are based primarily on data from the Hebrew bible and its versions (204).

[12] See, for example, E. Ullendorff, "Comparative Semitics," in *Linguistica Semitica: Presente e Futuro* (ed. G. Levi della Vida; Roma: Centro de Studi Semitici, 1961), who says, "In the 16th and 17th centuries Christian theologians and orientalists compared the vocabularies and verbal paradigms of Hebrew, Aramaic, Arabic, and Ethiopic, but most of them still considered Hebrew as the 'original' language, and any deviations from its 'pure' type were in the nature of 'corruptions'" (15).

dramatically in the eighteenth century when scholars began to recognize that these languages were to be seen as equal with, and not subordinate to, Hebrew. The person most responsible for this shift was A. Schultens (1686–1750), who initiated what has been termed a period of "hyperarabism" in Semitic studies. Hebrew began to lose its place of privilege in comparative work as a result of an increase in Arabic studies and a recognition of the great wealth of material found in the Arabic sources. Schultens' *Dissertatio Theologico-Philosophica de Utilitate Linguae Arabicae in Interpretanda Sacra Lingua*, written when he was twenty years old, was one of the first fruits of this new approach. D. Cohen explains its importance: "He announced that Arabic, Chaldean, Syriac and Ethiopic are sister languages to Hebrew in the same way that Aeolian, Ionian and Attic are to Greek. Above all, he called upon, by way of example, the abundant Arabic vocabulary to clarify the as yet obscure meanings of a part of the Hebrew vocabulary."[13]

This development began a new chapter in the study of comparative Semitics. The central position of Hebrew as the parent language was now being challenged by other languages, most notably Arabic. This led to a great flood of scholarly material which attempted to analyze Hebrew texts in light of the Arabic evidence. This method, signalling the displacement of Hebrew by Arabic as the primary Semitic language of comparison, remained the dominant one until recent times. It was only the discovery, decipherment and publication of materials written in Akkadian, Ugaritic and other related languages which caused a second methodological shift. Nonetheless, Arabic remains to the present day a resource of immense and indisputable value within comparative Semitics because of the unparalleled size and richness of its corpus.

Medieval Jewish Scholarship

Interest in the relationships among Semitic languages pre-dates the scholars and periods just discussed. Long before these efforts, others had engaged in work of a comparative nature. This work is of particular interest to us since it usually involved discussion of the relationship between Hebrew and Arabic.

There is evidence of attempts at etymologizing in the Bible, Talmud and midrashic literature of early Judaism. Some of these efforts make reference to languages related to Hebrew, but this cannot yet be considered comparative work in the true sense of the term. It is only in the tenth and eleventh centuries

[13] D. Cohen, 188.

that the resemblances among the various Semitic languages were critically noted and studied.

The first to recognize and explore the relationship between Hebrew and other languages were the Jewish scholars of the Middle Ages. This was due primarily to the context in which some of these scholars lived and worked. Those living outside of Palestine found themselves in situations that were "foreign" to Judaism and its traditions. Besides some of the obvious cultural differences of language and customs, there were differences of a scientific and religious nature that played a major role in the lives of these scholars and influenced the development of Jewish thought. Nowhere was this more evident than in the Arab world, and no scientific discipline was more affected by contact with the Arabs than linguistics. Arabic lexicography and grammar were among the first sciences to develop after the spread of Islam. It is therefore not surprising that Jewish lexicographers should have made use of the progress and results of their Arab counterparts in their study of Hebrew.

> There exists positive evidence that Arabic influence is visible even in the first efforts of Hebrew philology. For the Hebrew names of the principal vowels, *a, i, u,* and even the word for *vowel,* are mere translations from the Arabic. Moreover, the earliest works by Jews on the Hebrew language are not only written in Arabic, but arranged on the plan of their Arab models – adopting their terminology.[14]

By drawing upon the already well established work of Arab grammarians and lexicographers, Jewish scholars were able to begin the scientific study of Hebrew. In this way, we may speak of the medieval Jewish commentators as being among the first comparative Semitists in history.[15] We will now briefly examine the work of some of the more important figures of this period.

The pioneer and first great Jewish scholar in this tradition was Saᶜadiya (880–942), who was born in Egypt but spent most of his life in Babylonia, where he ended his career as the dean, or *gaon*, of the Babylonian academy at Sura. He composed a grammar and lexicon of biblical Hebrew, but only a few fragments have survived. His works on the Bible were important and influen-

[14] H. Hirschfeld, *Literary History of Hebrew Grammarians and Lexicographers* (Oxford: University Press, 1926) 7. This work, although now dated, is an excellent summary of the major figures of Hebrew grammar and lexicography.

[15] This point is made by E. L. Greenstein, "Medieval Bible Commentaries," in *Back to the Sources* (ed. B. W. Holtz; New York: Summit Books, 1984) 222.

tial, and his translation into Arabic remained the authoritative biblical text of many Arabic-speaking communities for centuries.

An analysis of the vocabulary and expressions which Saᶜadiya uses underscores the fact that his dependence upon Arabic was so pronounced that it sometimes goes against normal biblical usage and changes the meaning of passages. He sometimes translates terms in a typically Muslim way as when he prefers "*imam*" to "priest," uses "*caliph*" for "king," and translates "sanctuary" by "*miḥrāb*." The clearest example of this is in his remarks on Ps 80:14 when he uses the word "*Qur'ān*" as the equivalent for "Bible."

> The proper study of Hebrew begins with Saadiya. . . . His grammatical and lexicographical pioneering efforts laid the foundation for the many commentaries written in Spain, France and Germany. Saadiya is naturally influenced by Arab grammarians in his classification of Hebrew into nouns, verbs and particles, as also in his terminology.[16]

Ibn Qoreish was a mid-tenth century North African scholar who also exhibited keen awareness of comparative issues in his work. He wrote a letter to the Jews of Fez reminding them of the importance of using the Targum in their study of the Torah. It is composed of three sections. The first explores the relationship between Hebrew and Aramaic, the second examines alleged post-biblical words found in the Bible, and the last part of the work is concerned with a discussion of the relationship between Arabic and Hebrew. In the preface he gives a statement of his purpose, one with which most modern day comparative Semitists would agree: "I, therefore, resolved to write this book for intelligent readers that they may know that Aramaic and Arabic words, nay foreign and even Berber expressions are intermixed with the holy tongue, but Arabic in particular. For Arabic contains many words which we find to be pure Hebrew." Ibn Qoreish deserves to hold a central place in comparative Semitics on the basis of such statements and the tone of his work.

> It is not overstating the case if we style Ibn Qoreish the father of comparative Semitic philology, although such observation is spontaneous rather than founded on his scientific comprehension of the grammatical features of the

[16] E. I. J. Rosenthal, "Medieval Jewish Exegesis: its Character and Significance," *JSS* 9 (1966) 268. Rosenthal has written extensively on Saᶜadiya; see his "Saadya Gaon: An Appreciation of His Biblical Exegesis," *BJRL* 27 (1942) and "Saadya's Exegesis of the Book of Job," in *Saadya Studies* (ed. E. I. J. Rosenthal; Manchester: University Press, 1943). See also the collection of essays in L. Finkelstein, ed., *Rab Saadia Gaon: Studies in His Honor* (Jewish Theological Seminary of America, 1944).

> three languages. In this respect he surpassed his Arab teachers, who confined their linguistic studies to the most minute elaboration of the rules of their own language without acknowledging the existence of the kindred tongues.[17]

By the end of the tenth century, Babylonian Jewry had begun to decline and Spain became the primary center of cultural activity. Although this area had a strong Muslim and Christian presence, Jewish biblical scholarship thrived under the influence of Saʿadiya and Arabic linguistic studies. One scholar in particular was instrumental in establishing a solid foundation for the scientific study of Hebrew: Judah Ḥayyūj.

With Ḥayyūj, the study of Hebrew took a truly scientific form for the first time. Prior to this period Hebrew study was a field containing more speculation than insight. Ḥayyūj changed this dramatically. His chief contribution was the establishment of the triliteral theory of Hebrew roots and the application of this theory to weak verbs. In this way, he formulated rules for vowel changes and unusual forms, and solved many problems of the verbal system and morphology. All of his works were written in Arabic and employed the terminology of the Arab grammarians. Hirschfeld suggests that it was perhaps his familiarity with the Arabic language that enabled Ḥayyūj to unlock the mystery of the weak verbs and develop his theory of triliterality.

> The triliteral form of the roots of this language is much more conspicuous than in Hebrew, and had been recognized long before. Even in hollow roots the inaudible middle consonant is expressed orthographically by the letter of prolongation (ā), which, with very few exceptions, is absent in Hebrew. From the knowledge of the nature of roots consisting of three strong consonants to the examination of the weak ones was but one step, yet it required the sagacity of a genius to make this one step, and to discover that the long middle vowel in *qām* takes the place of the invisible radical letter.[18]

The work of Ḥayyūj was completed by Ibn Janāḥ, who was from Cordoba and died in the middle of the eleventh century. He disagreed with some of the conclusions reached by Ḥayyūj and wrote a supplementary work in which he added about fifty new roots not found in the earlier work while giving a different interpretation to a substantial number of others. His *magnum opus*, written later in his life, contained both a grammar (the first complete grammar

[17] Hirschfeld, 18–19.
[18] Hirschfeld, 35–36.

of Hebrew ever compiled) and a lexicon. Both of these have been preserved both in the original Arabic and in a Hebrew translation. Ibn Janāḥ called his grammar *Kitāb al-Lumaᶜ*, and the lexicon was simply titled *Kitāb al-Uṣūl* ("The Book of Roots").

Once again, with Ibn Janāḥ we see the central role Arabic played in elucidating Hebrew grammar and lexicography. Not only are his works written in Arabic, but he borrowed the standard arrangement of the Arabic grammars to structure his own Hebrew grammar. He also occasionally made use of Arabic terminology in his grammatical discussions in a way similar to some of his predecessors. In the preface to his book on grammar he clearly stated his dependence upon Arabic data whenever the Hebrew and Aramaic sources prove insufficient.

> If these should fail me I shall not hesitate to resort to Arabic, although some of my intelligent contemporaries forbear to do so. In this, too, I follow the example of Saadiya, who often translated a strange word with an Arabic one of similar sound. Our Rabbis also explained difficult words by similar ones in other languages.[19]

A final figure deserving mention for his importance in the development of comparative Semitics is the eleventh century Spanish Jew Ibn Barūn. His *Book of Comparison Between the Hebrew and Arabic Languages* was a careful treatment of the grammatical and lexical similarities between the two languages.[20] It is divided into two parts and our primary interest here is with the second, which is an alphabetically arranged lexicon of biblical roots with their Arabic equivalents.

In the course of his work, Ibn Barūn draws upon the efforts of his predecessors and makes reference to most of the significant figures of the past in both Hebrew and Arabic lexicography. In this way, he shows his familiarity with sources written in both languages.[21] The author he cites most frequently

[19] Quoted in Hirschfeld, 46.

[20] The work is extant only in fragmentary form. P. Wechter, *Ibn Barūn's Arabic Works on Hebrew Grammar and Lexicography* (Philadelphia: Dropsie College, 1964), follows Kokowzoff in attributing it to Ibn Barn, and considers it to be "the acme of comparative philological research attained by Jewish scholarship in Muslim Spain" (3). This book is an expansion of Wechter's earlier article, "Ibn Barūn's Contribution to Comparative Hebrew Philology," *JAOS* 61 (1941) 172–87.

[21] Wechter, *Ibn Barūn's Arabic Works*, lists the specific individuals and works that Ibn Barūn mentions on both the Hebrew (7) and Arabic (15) sides.

is Ibn Janāḥ, yet more than half the times he does so it is in a negative and critical way.

Perhaps the most valuable part of his work is the way he tries to categorize and list the similarities between the two languages as they are found in individual words. This is significant because it is the first systematic attempt to articulate the laws governing the lexical similarities of Hebrew and Arabic. He identifies seven related categories or aspects: 1) words showing a similarity in orthography, pronunciation and meaning, 2) words showing a similarity due to interchange of homo-organic letters, 3) words showing a similarity due to interchange of letters contiguous in the alphabet, 4) words showing a similarity because of metathesis, 5) words showing a similarity because of errors in orthography, 6) similarity between words with meanings that are diametrically opposed, and 7) words showing a similarity in meaning but not in pronunciation.[22]

It is important to note the key role geography played in these early attempts at discussing the relationship between Hebrew and Arabic. The Jewish scholars in Arabic speaking lands had better potential to become proto-comparative Semitists since they were familiar with Arabic, biblical Hebrew, rabbinic Hebrew and Aramaic. Those scholars who did not know Arabic, therefore, were working at a disadvantage since they did not have access to either the original work of the Arab grammarians or the later Jewish commentaries which were based on Arabic sources and were written in that language.

> Jews who studied Arabic language and literature, as well as other academic disciplines, learned the new linguistic science and desired to exploit it in their exegesis of the Bible and the analysis of Hebrew grammar. Only those who knew Arabic grammar developed the proper understanding of the Hebrew verb as a stem built upon three consonants. . . . Characteristic of the Spanish Jewish scholars was their superior interest and training in linguistic analysis, a benefit of having grown up in an Arabic milieu.[23]

This survey of the more important biblical commentators of medieval Judaism has highlighted the great importance of Arabic in the development of Jewish lexicography and grammar. The work and insights of Arab scholars were a major influence on those who gave shape and direction to Hebrew linguistics. This influence becomes most apparent when we note the state of

[22] Examples which Ibn Barūn gives for each of these types are found in Wechter, *Ibn Barūn's Arabic Works*, 54–56.

[23] Greenstein, 222.

affairs in those places that did not have access to the Arabic material. Hebrew lexicography in parts of Europe that could not draw directly upon the Arabic sources was not marked by the same creativity and vitality that the Near East and Spain witnessed. We must now turn to see who these Arabic thinkers were and why they had such a profound and far-reaching effect on the world around them.

Arabic Lexicography

Lexicography (*ʿilm al-luġa*), along with grammar and rhetoric, is one of the three divisions which the Arabs established in their early scientific study of linguistics.[24] These disciplines were held in such high regard that they were placed at the pinnacle of the philological sciences. "It is already a sign of a fertile inner attitude toward the language when the authors of the Arabic tongue award grammar (*naḥw*) and lexicography (*luġa*) a special, and occasionally even the first, rank among the cultural sciences (*ʿulūm al-ʾadab*)."[25]

Several points are important regarding the history of Arabic dictionaries. First of all, among the languages of the world perhaps only Chinese contains an earlier example of a true dictionary. More than a dozen good dictionaries existed in Arabic at a time when such works were practically nonexistent in Europe. Secondly, the attempt at comprehensiveness and inclusion of all words in the language which was characteristic of them set the early Arabic dictionaries apart from those of other languages. "In this, they differed from the earlier lexicographers of other nations, whose chief aim was to explain rare and difficult words."[26] A third important point to keep in mind is that the outward form and organizing principles of Arabic dictionaries changed significantly over the centuries. This will become apparent as we now examine some of the more important examples of Arabic dictionaries and the figures behind them.

[24] S. Wild, *Das Kitāb al-ʿAin und die arabische Lexikographie* (Wiesbaden: Harrassowitz, 1965) 1–3, notes this division in his perceptive study of the origin of Arabic lexicography. Two other works which offer fine discussions of the development of Arabic lexicography are Wild's "Arabische Lexicographie" in *Grundriß der arabischen Philologie 2* (ed. H. Gätje; Wiesbaden: Harrassowitz, 1987) and F. Sezgin, *Geschichte des arabischen Schriftums VII* (Leiden: Brill, 1982).

[25] H. Gätje, "Arabische Lexikographie," *Bustan* 5 (1964) 3.

[26] J. A. Haywood, *Arabic Lexicography* (Leiden: Brill, 1965) 2. Haywood's first chapter offers an excellent summary of pre-Arab lexicography. Hsü Shen's *Shuo Wen*, written in China at the end of the first century C.E., is singled out as the first true extant dictionary. (6)

The first true Arab lexicographer was al-Khalīl Ibn-Ahmad (c. 718–790). As just mentioned, an analysis of the history of Arabic lexicography shows a clear development in the form of the dictionary. Three distinct stages, differentiated by the way they organize and present the material, can be discerned. The *Kitāb al-ᶜAin* of al-Khalīl, besides being the prototype of all Arabic dictionaries, is also the most representative example of the first of these types.[27]

The organizing principle and structure of the dictionary are carefully described and explained in the book's preface.[28] There we learn that the material is broken down into individual chapters for each letter of the alphabet. These chapters are presented in a phonetic arrangement, beginning with the innermost sound of the set of letters/sounds in terms of point of articulation and moving outward to the labials. The dictionary therefore begins with the letter *ᶜain* (hence its name) and ends with *mīm*. The chapters get progressively shorter since not only roots which begin with a particular letter are included in a particular chapter but any roots which contain the letter. A further organizing principle of the *Kitāb al-ᶜAin* is that it is anagrammatically arranged with all permutations of any given group of letters being grouped together (for instance, *madda* occurs with *damma*).[29]

The work of al-Khalīl was the foundation and model for all later efforts at writing an Arabic dictionary. For the present study the dictionaries of six of al-Khalīl's best known and most frequently cited successors have been chosen as the primary authorities which will be consulted in discussing and interpreting Arabic data in later chapters. They constitute a representative group which spans the entire history of Arabic lexicography.

Arabic Dictionaries Consulted

1) The Jamhara *of Ibn Duraid*

The second attempt to write an exhaustive dictionary in Arabic was undertaken by Ibn Duraid (837–934), who compiled his *Al-Jamhara fīl-Luğa* ("The Collection in the Language") in Persia. He used many of al-Khalīl's ideas and reworked others. In agreement with his predecessor, roots were arranged in an anagrammatical fashion with all possible combinations of the root letters listed together and these were grouped according to the number of their let-

[27] This tripartite division of the dictionaries by type is reflected in the study of Haywood.

[28] A complete translation of this preface may be found in Haywood, 28–37.

[29] A good summary of the order and structure of al-Khalīl's dictionary is given in Gätje, 7.

ters. He differed from al-Khalīl, however, in his use of the normal letter order of the Arabic alphabet.

A further departure is seen in the way the two chose to divide the material. As we have seen, al-Khalīl used the letters of the alphabet as a way of marking the chapters in his dictionary. Ibn Duraid, on the other hand, used the number of radical letters as the basis for his division. This had disastrous results. The work becomes increasingly confusing as overlapping and repetition occur. Without the helpful index which modern editions include, consulting this dictionary would be an extremely frustrating and time-consuming exercise.

2) The Tahḏīb *of Al-Azharī*

Another lexicographer who followed al-Khalīl's anagrammatic method is al-Azharī (895–981) whose *Tahḏīb fīl-Luġa* ("A Refinement in the Language") is significant because it was a valuable source for the *Lisān al-ʿArab*. It also contains an account of the history of Arabic lexicography which is a very useful source of information. One contribution al-Azharī made to al-Khalīl's work is the addition of numerous literary quotations and citations which support the meanings proposed in the dictionary. These often prove invaluable in determining the historical development of an Arabic form or meaning.

3) The Ṣiḥāḥ *of Al-Jauharī*

The anagrammatical structure which al-Khalīl introduced remained the typical dictionary arrangement for two centuries. It was only in the late tenth century that a new method emerged which was based on rhyme. The person responsible for this shift was al-Jauharī (d. 1007), whose *Tāj al Luġa wa Ṣiḥāḥ al-ʿArabīyya* ("The Crown of Language and the Correct of Arabic") became the standard Arabic dictionary for three hundred years. His work contained twenty-eight chapters, one for each letter, which were arranged in the order of the alphabet. Roots were grouped according to their last radical letter so that all roots ending in a particular letter were found in the same chapter. Haywood points out the advantages, both practical and social, this system had over the more complicated arrangement used prior to this.

> The *Ṣaḥāḥ* or *Ṣiḥāḥ* was the first Arabic dictionary to be so arranged according to a single simple system as to be a useful reference work for the ordinary layman unskilled in Arabic philological science. It came at a time when it was

> badly needed – when the fragments of the empire of the Caliphs could no longer be termed "Arab" even in a loose sense, and when the general standard of proficiency in Arabic must have been low.[30]

In the preface to his work al-Jauharī identifies its two key features: it introduces a new arrangement and includes only "correct" words which are typically found in Arabic speech. We have already noted the first feature. The second was the factor toward which much of the criticism levelled at his dictionary was directed. In his desire to limit his efforts to what he considered to be proper and conventional Arabic, al-Jauharī may have omitted a great deal.[31]

The dictionary of al-Jauharī represented a significant step forward in Arabic lexicography. It was only later, when the requirements and qualities of a good dictionary changed, that the work was surpassed by others. However, the value and influence of the *Ṣiḥāḥ* can be seen in the fact that many of its successors continued to use its rhyme arrangement as their organizing principle.

> The importance of the *Ṣiḥāḥ* is exemplified by the fact that its arrangement was imitated by the succeeding lexicographers. It ceased to be the standard work only when the *Lisān* and *Qāmūs* appeared. These were more suited to a later age which required a large and exhaustive dictionary, and which was not interested in any purist's endeavour to exclude incorrect or non-Arabic words.[32]

4) The Lisān *of Ibn Manẓūr*

The *Lisān al-ʿArab* ("The Tongue of the Arabs") was compiled by the Tunisian Ibn Manẓūr (1232–1311), who was sometimes known as Ibn Mukarram. It was an attempt to give a comprehensive, almost exhaustive, account of the Arabic vocabulary. Ibn Manẓūr states that his main purpose was to replace all earlier dictionaries by drawing from them.[33] To do this he recorded every

[30] Haywood, 70. He also remarks that although al-Jauharī is usually credited with having introduced the rhyme order into Arabic lexicography it had already been used by both the Jewish scholar Saʿadiya and al-Jauharī's uncle Abū Ibrāhīm al-Fārābī (d. 980). Nonetheless, the *Ṣiḥaḥ* is the first comprehensive use of the method.

[31] This is perhaps best seen in the fact that al-Sağānī (1177–1262), who attempted to fill in some of these gaps in his *Takmila* ("Completion") of the *Ṣiḥaḥ*, added some 60,000 new entries to the earlier work.

[32] Haywood, 76.

[33] This operating principle was followed slavishly in the work and underlines the fact that Ibn Manẓūr was primarily a compiler and not a scholar of great original insight. He was usually con-

root he was able to identify, along with every derivation of each root, and illustrated them with numerous examples and references. The result was a listing of 80,000 roots and their derivatives. This was the most extensive Arabic dictionary yet seen, and one that may have only been surpassed by some Chinese lexicographers.

The *Lisān* is structured in the rhyme arrangement of al-Jauharī. This choice is interesting in light of the fact that prior to this a number of other dictionaries had appeared which made use of the modern order based on the first letters of the words.[34]

Perhaps the only major drawback of the work is the one which plagued many of its predecessors: a lack of organization in the listing of derived forms. There is no one standard system that is used throughout the entire dictionary and under a given root verbs, verbal nouns and adjectives may appear in any order. Nonetheless, the *Lisān al-ᶜArab* is a monumental work of immense importance that continues until the present day to be the major reference work for many educated Arabs. "The reading of any of the longer articles in the *Lisān* is a linguistic and literary experience. It gives us glimpses into a whole world of Arabic culture."[35]

The sheer size of the *Lisān* proved to be a major drawback. Its bulk made it impractical to use for many and too costly for others.[36] It was therefore inevitable that sooner or later someone would attempt to compile a dictionary of more manageable proportions that did not greatly sacrifice the comprehensiveness of Ibn Manẓūr's work. This goal was realized in the *al-Qāmūs al-Muḥīṭ* of al-Fīrūzābādī (1326–1414).[37]

---

tent to simply repeat word for word what his predecessors had stated in their works. This is taken to an extreme degree at times when he reproduces side by side the contradictory views of two earlier lexicographers.

[34] Haywood (80) believes that the reason for this may lie in the fact that the works that did adopt the modern order were, for the most part, shorter lists treating specialized vocabulary like religious language and legal terminology. The only two options available for the type of comprehensive work Ibn Manẓūr undertook were the anagrammatic approach of al-Khalīl and the rhyme arrangement of al-Jauharī.

[35] Haywood, 82.

[36] The Beirut edition of 1955–56 comprises 15 volumes, each having about 500 double-columned pages.

[37] To al-Fīrūzābādī goes the honor of having first used the term (*Qāmūs*) which subsequently came to mean "dictionary" and is still used as such today.

5) The Qāmūs of Al-Fīrūzābādī

While the *Lisān* is the dictionary that is kept in the library and preferred by scholars, the *al-Qāmūs al-Muḥīṭ* ("The Surrounding Ocean") is found in the home and is the primary reference work for the average Arabic reader. Al-Fīrūzābādī was a master of brevity and the use of abbreviations. He consulted many other works in the course of his compilation but made no reference to them in his dictionary. In the same way, he did away with most of the literary and illustrative examples. In a further effort to save space, he introduced a series of sigla and abbreviations which cover points of grammar, vocalization, and geography and give other information to the user. The net result is a dictionary which, in two volumes, is much shorter than Ibn Manẓūr's but, with 60,000 entries, is almost as comprehensive. The rhyme order was chosen by Al-Fīrūzābādī for his own work. This choice appears to be a deliberate one in light of the fact that, as was the case with Ibn Manẓūr who wrote earlier, the modern arrangement based on the first letter of words was already known and used.

An interesting quality of the *Qāmūs* is its polemical attitude toward the earlier work of al-Jauharī. Although al-Fīrūzābādī adopted the rhymed order of the *Ṣiḥāḥ*, he saw his work as a corrective to his predecessor's, which he believed was too selective and omitted a great range of vocabulary which was important. To highlight this point, al-Fīrūzābādī wrote in red ink all of the material which the *Ṣiḥāḥ* left out and which he included. He asserted that he had not done this in a boastful way, but it caused a division within the field of lexicography and generated a debate between those who supported al-Jauharī and those who favored al-Fīrūzābādī. "This, it must be confessed, al-Fīrūzābādī had called down upon himself, not only by his flamboyant display of his predecessor's omissions in red ink, but by pointing out the latter's errors here and there."[38]

6) The Tāj *of Al-Zabīdī*

Another dictionary written in the rhyme arrangement which will be frequently cited in this study is the *Tāj al-ʿArūs min jawāhīr al-Qāmūs* ("The Crown of the Bride from the Jewels of the *Qāmūs*") of al-Zabīdī (1732–1791). This is an expansion of the *Qāmūs* which drew upon most of the older works

[38] Haywood, 87.

and dictionaries and resulted in the largest Arabic dictionary ever compiled. With 120,000 entries it doubled the size of the *Qāmūs*. Following the standard practice which set off the original text in published editions al-Zabīdī enclosed the contents of the *Qāmūs* in brackets and added other material, including new roots, new derivations under already existing roots, amplifications, quotations and the mention of authorities. This work achieved much fame and importance as the primary source for the lexicon of Lane, whose tale of his quest for it is a fascinating story.[39]

The third type of dictionary, and the last to reach its most fully developed form, is that written in the modern arrangement which organizes its material in alphabetical order according to the first letter of the root. The alphabetic order of the letters was known and accepted as far back as al-Khalīl and the early days of Arabic lexicography. However, as we have seen, for linguistic and scientific reasons he and his successors preferred not to use it as the organizing principle in their work. It was the Persian scholar Ibn Fāris (d. 1005) who first used the modern arrangement in a systematic and comprehensive way in his *al-Mujmal*.[40] Another work of Ibn Fāris that will be cited frequently in the course of this study is his *Maqāyīs al-Luḡa* ("The Standards of the Language"). his lexicon is dedicated to the meanings of consonantal roots. It lists the number and meanings of the semantic bases for each root in a clear, concise way which is less confusing than what is often found in the dictionaries mentioned above.

European Arabic Dictionaries

The above survey has indicated some of the major works and figures in the history of Arabic lexicography. This listing would be incomplete if some men-

[39] Edward W. Lane, *Arabic-English Lexicon* (Beirut: Librairie du Liban, 1980) xviii–xxi. Originally published in 1863-93 (London: Williams & Norgate).

[40] There are a number of works prior to this that make some use of the alphabetic arrangement, but they cannot really be called true prototypes of the modern dictionary. Representatives of this group include the *Kitāb al-Jīm* of Abū ʿAmr (d. 825) and the *Kitāb al-Maqsūr wa al-Mamdūd* of Ibn Wallād (d. 834). Although they group words into twenty eight chapters according to the first letter of the root, within the chapters the words are arranged either randomly or according to some yet unknown principle. They are also specialized vocabularies rather than full dictionaries. The first treats primarily rare words and the dialects of some desert tribes and the second deals with words ending in the letter *alif* (Haywood, 92–98).

tion were not made of the European orientalists whose efforts made the information contained in these dictionaries available to a wider audience outside the Arab world. For the most part, these scholars translated older works and used them as the basis for their own dictionaries. While they display very little that is new on the level of content, these European works did modify and improve upon the form of their sources. The clearest way this was done was in their adoption of the modern dictionary arrangement for works that had been compiled in the anagrammatic or rhyme format.

The first European to put together an Arabic lexicon was Jacobus Golius (1596–1667), whose one-volume *Lexicon Arabico-Latinum* was published in 1653. It was based primarily on the *Ṣiḥāḥ* of al-Jauharī, but he also referred to other works including the *Qāmūs*. This was the major reference work for European Arabic studies for almost two hundred years.

The dictionary that replaced it was Georg Wilhelm Freytag's *Lexicon Arabico-Latinum*, a four-volume work published between 1830 and 1837. This was basically a translation of the *Qāmūs*, although Freytag also consulted Golius and the *Ṣiḥāḥ*. The shortcoming of this dictionary was the same as that of its source, the *Qāmūs*: it simply listed words and their meanings and did not support or illustrate the definitions through literary examples. This was a serious drawback for European students who needed more data to fully understand the meanings of rare words.

The work of Edward William Lane tried to remedy this situation. His eight-volume *English-Arabic Lexicon*, published between 1863 and 1893, is a very detailed and carefully researched work which gives definitions in English instead of Latin, as Freytag and Golius had. "It is difficult to conceive a better dictionary in the accuracy of its definitions, and the fullness of its examples. It is surely one of the finest dictionaries ever written in any language."[41] As mentioned earlier, Lane's lexicon was based on the *Tāj al-ʿArūs* of al-Zabīdī.

An important aspect of Lane's work is the fact that he never finished the lexicon. The last two volumes were published by his nephew after his death, and they are simply the text of Lane's notes as he was preparing the material before he had a chance to supplement them and expand upon them. Volumes seven and eight, therefore, are not of the same high quality as the earlier volumes and the lexicon is not a very reliable tool after the entry for the root *qadda*. Spitaler points out the positive and negative features of Lane's dictionary: "It surpasses its predecessors through its many exact renderings of meanings, explanations

[41] Haywood, 125.

and proofs. However, it restricts itself to what Lane and the scholarly community of the time determined to be properly common vocabulary. In addition, it is only a torso which reaches to somewhere in the middle of the letter *qāf*."[42]

An attempt to supplement Lane's lexicon was made by R. P. A. Dozy, who published his *Supplément aux Dictionnaires Arabes* in 1881. This two-volume work includes many words and meanings which are not found in Lane's dictionary and it is frequently cited by Hebraists discussing Arabic cognates to Hebrew roots. Dozy's dictionary must be used with caution, however, since much of the material it contains comes from Arab Spain. Evidence from Dozy must therefore be carefully studied to determine its role within the wider context of the Arabic language and its relevance for the biblical period.[43]

Another European dictionary which deserves special mention is Adolf Wahrmund's *Handwörterbuch der neu-arabischen und deutschen Sprache*, published in 1898. This is a reliable resource which is based on the Turkish translation of the *Qāmūs* and contains much ancient material.

Finally, we must also note the existence of a great number of shorter Arabic dictionaries which give meanings in European languages. These typically cover the usage of a particular region and/or period and their main purpose is to give the non-native speaker the translation of Arabic words in a language with which he or she is familiar. Accordingly, these works do not contain adequate information regarding such issues as the lexical history and semantic development of forms and meanings. Since such information is vital when proposing suggestions regarding the relevance of the Arabic data for biblical Hebrew these resources are of no real help for scholars and, consequently,

[42] Anton Spitaler, "Arabisch," in *Linguistica Semitica: Presente e Futuro* (ed. G. Levi della Vida; Roma: Centro di Studi Semitici, 1961) 129.

[43] This point will be treated in more depth in a later chapter. Another noteworthy and more recent attempt to supplement Lane's lexicon was begun in 1957 by J. Kraemer, A. Spitaler and H. Gätje with the publication of the first fascicle of their *Wörterbuch der Klassischen Arabischen Sprache* (Wiesbaden: Harrassowitz, 1957). The name first associated with this project was A. Fischer who, at the time of his death during the Second World War, had over 350,000 slips of paper containing material from literary and religious sources not found in the older dictionaries. In keeping with their intention to supplement Lane, Kraemer and Gätje started their dictionary with the letter *kāf*. After Kraemer's death M. Ullmann got involved with the project, which is far from complete. As of 1991 twenty fascicles had been published through the root *lky*. At this rate, completion of the project is still a long way off. For an account of the work of Fischer and its results see J. Kraemer, "August Fischers Sammlungen zum Arabischen Lexicon," *ZDMG* 105 (1955) 81–85. For further information on the history of this project see Haywood (125–26, 137) and Spitaler (130–31).

should not be consulted. Unfortunately, in practice scholars often base their proposals on these questionable sources.[44]

Among those consulted, two deserve special mention since they appear with some regularity in the work of biblical scholars. H. Wehr's *A Dictionary of Modern Written Arabic* is a popular resource which can be easily acquired but, as its title indicates, it is concerned only with the modern literary form of the language. It is consequently of no use for Hebraists working with the biblical material. More frequently cited is J. G. Hava's *Arabic-English Dictionary*, which was originally published in the early part of this century but is available in later editions. Although it contains some ancient material there are also many modern forms and meanings interspersed throughout. Because there is often no precise way of determining what is modern and what is older this is not a reliable source.

Description of the Present Study

Hebraists have, of course, made use of the Arabic dictionaries in their study of Hebrew lexicography and have based many of their conclusions on the data which they contain. As mentioned earlier, much of what they have proposed has been carefully researched and has furthered our understanding of the biblical material and deepened our insight into the relationship between Arabic and Hebrew. But other efforts have been less than satisfactory from the point of view of both methodology and results. One of the primary reasons for this is the uncritical way in which some have used the resources for Arabic. Because they have not been aware of the shortcomings and limitations of the dictionaries they have consulted, or have chosen to ignore the difficulties, their conclusions and proposals are sometimes inaccurate and misleading. The time has come to examine the use of Arabic in biblical Hebrew lexicography in order to evaluate its effectiveness in the past and plot its course for the future.

Each of the next three chapters will discuss a particular type of error often found among scholars who refer to the Arabic sources in their work in biblical Hebrew lexicography. These three types of errors have all been labelled and described in ways which emphasize a person's vision and ability to see. This comes out clearly in the terms that are used to categorize the three types: tunnel vision, myopia, and astigmatism. This terminology highlights the fact that, in most cases, it is a scholar's inability to properly see and perceive the

[44] This practice and the resulting problems will be discussed repeatedly in the course of this study.

Arabic data that leads to errors in analysis and interpretation. Those who exhibit symptoms of tunnel vision focus too exclusively on only one relatively minor portion of the available data on an Arabic form and do not take into account the wider semantic range. Scholars who are prone to myopia are unable to extend their field of vision far back enough in the historical development of the Arabic language and, consequently, base their conclusions on evidence which is representative of only one period and/or place along the continuum of that development. Those experiencing astigmatism suffer from an inability to focus clearly on the data presented in the Arabic sources, which then leads to a distorted perception of the data and the advancement of suggestions that have no genuine basis. For each type of error, specific examples of these mistakes will be identified and analyzed in detail with particular attention paid to the importance of proper and careful use of the original Arabic sources. A brief concluding chapter will offer some preliminary guidelines for those who wish to make more effective use of Arabic in biblical Hebrew lexicography.

A final point is in order regarding the question of the scholars who are cited in this work. It will be apparent that certain names, particularly those of G. R. Driver and A. Guillaume, appear with great frequency. This is so because of their familiarity with the Arabic sources and their relative proficiency in the language compared with other Hebrew Bible scholars. They have therefore been extremely prolific in their proposals involving the use of Arabic in biblical Hebrew. They have made many worthwhile contributions and the frequent citation of them here is not meant to denigrate those contributions. Given their incredible productivity in the field of comparative lexicography certain problems are bound to appear. The intent of the present work is to foster the use of Arabic in biblical Hebrew lexicography by identifying the mistakes one needs to avoid to more profitably engage in such comparative work.

CHAPTER 2

Restricting the Semantic Range: Tunnel Vision

Very few languages can rival Arabic in terms of its capacity for polyvalence and its position as a storehouse of data in which a variety of seemingly unrelated, even conflicting, meanings for the same word are able to coexist. This characteristic is both a blessing and a curse. It has the advantage of endowing the language with such a vast reservoir of resources from which to draw that it makes the potential for expression seem almost limitless. This is particularly effective in the area of poetry and other forms of artistic composition. On the down side, this tendency toward multiple denotation can give the impression that Arabic is a language that is undefined, ambiguous and capricious. This is frequently the sentiment of non-native speakers who work with Arabic, and is often expressed in one of two ways: paralysis or hyperactivity.

On the one hand, the sheer volume of data and the dizzying range of available choices can freeze one and cause immobility as the daunting task is faced of discerning what the proper meaning of a word might be in a given context. There are, on the other hand, those who revel in the diversity and richness that is the Arabic language. They take great delight in the opportunity for creativity and activity that the many options offer to them as they range far and wide over available meanings.

In their work with Arabic, biblical Hebrew scholars have more often fallen into the second category than the first. Because their primary concern has been to illuminate the text, they have not hesitated to comb the cognate sources, Arabic included, until they have uncovered the one meaning that gives the word its proper nuance and furnishes the key to interpretation. While this approach has proven valuable in many cases and is preferred to that of the paralytic, it is not without its dangers.

A common problem that one encounters may perhaps best be described as a form of tunnel vision. As mentioned above, the definitions for a particular word are frequently many and varied. Quite often, once a particular one has been decided upon by a searching scholar, all others, especially those that are unrelated or opposed to it, recede into the scholar's background. Usually, the other meanings do not enter into the scholar's discussion at all. This presents no problem as long as the choice has been made with care and is methodologically sound. However, there are many pitfalls, and the choice of one particular meaning may be based on an incomplete or inaccurate reading of the Arabic material and thereby give a distorted picture of the data. The scholar may be blind to, or choose to ignore, the wider context of the Arabic root/word under discussion. This scholarly tunnel vision usually takes one of three different forms:

1) Isolation of a Rare/Secondary Meaning

Sometimes a scholar will propose a reading of a Hebrew word that is based on a cognate Arabic word although study of the Arabic dictionaries shows that the meaning selected is not the basic or primary meaning of the word. On occasion, the definition given is extremely secondary and its accuracy open to some doubt. The Arabic meaning has been isolated and given far greater importance than the evidence allows.[1]

2) Reliance Upon a Single Source

On occasion a scholar will put forth an Arabic meaning which is found in only one source. Sometimes this one source is a dictionary (usually one of the less important ones) and at other times it is simply a quotation or citation from

[1] The relationship of rare or secondary meanings to semantic bases of consonantal roots is a complex problem. The Arabs' delight in language is conspicuous, even from pre-Islamic times, and the influence of metaphor and the spread of extended usages in the common lexicon is pervasive. Similarly, sensitivity to the semantic possibilities of morphological patterns is considerable so that the free use of verbal and nominal derivatives based on nouns, adjectives and verbs is universal. Because many of these developments are predictable or immediately understandable to the native speaker they are not noted by the lexicographers and philologians. This can frequently make the determination of the relationship of a particular meaning to other meanings a complicated task.

some historical figure. If none of the standard dictionaries or lexicons contain the meaning, this seriously undermines the validity and relevance of the comparison.

3) Disregard for the Semantic Field

There are instances in which an individual meaning for a root/word is not discussed in terms of the larger context of the entire semantic field of the root or the word. This error can sometimes take the form of an improper extension of meaning. Arabic senses that are well established are occasionally stretched by scholars to better support their positions. This lack of understanding regarding how the word/root functions in the wider semantic context easily leads to a treatment and analysis that is unavoidably distorted.

The following are examples of each of these more common types of tunnel vision which can befall biblical scholars as they make use of the Arabic data in their studies.[2]

1) Isolation of a Rare/Secondary Meaning

2.1.1. BḎʾ I, *baḏaʾa, yabḏaʾu // bāzāʾ*[3]

The Hebrew verb *bāzāʾ* is found only in Isaiah 18, where it appears twice (vv 2, 7). Both times it is in the third person plural *Qal* form, with the word "rivers" as subject. The word has been a crux for translators and interpreters.[4] G. R. Driver has proposed the Arabic verb *baḏaʾa* as a cognate, which he claims supports the reading "whose land is scoured by rivers."[5] A problem exists with

[2] Scholars have occasionally pointed out the problems inherent in approaches which isolate an Arabic meaning from its context thereby drawing inappropriate conclusions which are then applied to other Semitic languages. For an early attempt to debunk a proposed Arabic etymology see S. Moscati, "The 'Aramean Ahlamu'," *JSS* 4 (1959) 303–7. For neglect of considering all derivations from an Arabic root and the resulting biased and unrealistic results see G. Krotkoff, "*Laḥm* 'Fleisch' und *leḥem* 'Brot'," *WZKM* 62 (1969) 76–82.

[3] The heading of each form treated will contain the following information in order: the letters of the Arabic root, a Roman numeral indicating which conjugation of the Arabic verb is being discussed, the masculine third person singular forms of both the perfect and imperfect tenses in that conjugation, and the Hebrew form to which it is being compared. For nominal forms, only the Arabic root letters and the noun are given.

[4] The lack of certainty is reflected in the various ways the word has been translated: "spoiled" (*KJV*), "scoured" (*NEB*, *REB*), "washed" (*NAB*), "criss-crossed" (*NJB*), and "divide" (*NRSV*) are representative examples.

[5] G. R. Driver, "Isaiah I–XXXIX: Textual and Linguistic Problems," *JSS* 13 (1968) 46. This is the reading that is adopted in the *NEB* text. Driver was a very influential member of the *NEB* team

this suggestion since the Arabic verb never actually means "scour."[6] When referring to land the verb typically denotes not "scour," but becoming unfruitful and devoid of pasture.[7] It appears that perhaps Driver has focused upon this possible contextual sense, which is not the primary meaning of the root, to bolster his suggestion, which, he observes, is in line with the meaning "pillaged" found in the versions. A further challenge to his proposal may also be noted. Because the Arabic evidence speaks of lack of pasture and fertility when this root refers to land, Driver must also somehow explain how a land's rivers can be the source of its barrenness.

2.1.2. ḤLQ I, *ḥalaqa, yaḥliqu // ḥālāq*

D. J. Kamhi has proposed this Arabic root, to which he assigns the meaning "high," to help explain the Hebrew word *ḥālāq*, which is twice found after the word "mountain" in the book of Joshua (11:17, 12:7).[8] While there is some evidence to support this contention, a closer look at the sources points up the secondary nature of the meaning. The primary meaning of the Arabic root has to do with roundness and the shape of a circle, as seen in derivations which describe a hill and a full udder. A further sense, which is well attested and appears in various forms, is related to the idea of shaving and the removal of hair. This may be connected to the primary sense through the circular movements of the sharp object which produce a smooth, round surface. Words within this root can refer to the drawing of a circle, a brand in the form of a ring, the halo of the moon, people sitting in a circle, etc. Certain body parts

---

and in 1965 became one of its directors. It will be noted in the course of this study that a number of his translations which are, like this one, based on the Arabic evidence either found their way into the text or were accepted as alternative readings. In some of these cases the Arabic data he cites cannot sustain his position or support his claim.

[6] The more basic meaning of the root appears to be one of being disliked or hated.

[7] See, for example, al-Azharī's quote of Abū ʿUbaida's definition "he (a human subject) found fault with the land as (far as its quality as) a pasture (goes)" in his (Azharī's) *Al-Tahḏīb fīl-Luġa* (Cairo: Dār al-Miṣrīya lil-Taʾlīf wal-Tarjama, 1964) 15, 24. There is, in fact, no mention of rivers or water in any of the major Arabic dictionaries consulted in this study: Ibn Duraid's *Al-Jamhara fīl-Luġa* (Hayderabad: Oriental Publications Bureau, 1926), al-Jauharī's *Al-Ṣiḥāḥ* (Beirut: Dār al-Ḥaḍāra al-ʿArabīya, 1974) 1. 78; Ibn Manẓūr's *Lisān al-ʿArab* (Cairo: Dār al-Miṣrīya lil-Taʾlīf wal-Tarjama, 1966) 1. 22; al-Fīrūzābādī's *Al-Qāmūs al-Muḥīṭ* (Beirut: al-Muʾassasa al-ʿArabīya lil-Ṭibāʿa wal-Našr, 1970) 1. 8; al-Zabīdī's *Tāj al-ʿArūs* (Libya, n.d.) 1. 44; Lane's *Arabic-English Lexicon* (London, 1863–93; reprinted, Beirut: Librarie du Liban, 1980) 172–73. Ibn Fāris' *Maqāyīs al-Luġa* (Cairo: al-Dār al-Islāmīya, 1990) 1. 217 says that it refers to the inability to praise a place and this is clearly related to the basic meaning "to dislike" which he identifies.

[8] D. J. Kamhi, "The Root *ḥlq* in the Bible," *VT* 23 (1973) 239.

which are round in shape are also found under this root, including the throat and the openings of the anus and vulva.[9]

The verbal forms of the root usually associated with height seem to be related to this sense of "roundness." This is seen in its use to describe a bird circling in the sky and the round sun making its way from one end of the sky to the other.[10] There are a few sources which speak simply of height with no reference to circling, but this is clearly secondary to the root and may be a later development.[11] If one wishes to consult this Arabic root for support regarding this Hebrew word, it seems better to draw upon the more basic meaning of shaving and give it the sense of "bare" or "bald" as the NEB has done.[12] The nominal forms of the Arabic root seem to point in this direction as well. When the word *ḥāliq* refers to a mountain (among its many other possible meanings), it indicates one that has no vegetation upon it.[13]

2.1.3. ḎYʿ I, *ḏāʿa, yaḏīʿu // mazîaʿ*

According to G. R. Driver, the primary significance of the Semitic root *ḏāʿa* is one of extravagance or excessive self-indulgence and this is clearly seen in such Arabic expressions as "the people or camels drank all that was in the watering trough or tank."[14] He attempts to link this Arabic root and meaning with the word *mazîaʿ* in Sir 37:30. Driver notes that the context, which contains several references to overeating and gluttony, suggests a meaning along these lines.

There are two weaknesses apparent in Driver's method and conclusion. In

[9] See Lane, 628–30; *Ṣiḥāḥ* 1. 290–91; *Jamhara* 2. 180; *Tāj* 3. 19–21.

[10] Al-Azharī (*Tahḏīb* 4. 63–64) quotes some authorities which support the notion that it is the circling and not the height which is primary to the meaning. One says that the moon *taḥallaqa* if it circles in its orbit. Another usage which highlights more clearly the difference between circling and height in the root describes the verb as the action of a man who scans the heavens as the bird circles (*yuḥalliq*) when it goes up (*irtafaʿa*) in the air.

[11] See, for example, the *Maqāyīs* (2. 98–99), which lists "to be high" as the third of the three basic senses of the root which are identified, following those referring to shaving and roundness.

[12] This is, in fact, the meaning given to the word in M. Koehler and W. Baumgartner, *Hebräisches und Aramäisches Lexicon zum Alten Testament* (Leiden: E. J. Brill, 1967–1990) 310. This lexicon will hereafter be referred to as *HALAT*.

[13] A further, contextual factor works against Kamhi's translation of this word as "high." In both places in Joshua it is immediately followed by the word *ʿōleh*, which already carries the sense of height. While such use of back-to-back synonyms is not impossible in biblical Hebrew, it does seem a bit odd. The fact that all other occurrences of the Hebrew root suggest smoothness, coupled with the Arabic evidence, seems to point in the direction of a translation along the lines of the one cited above (*NEB*).

[14] G. R. Driver, "Supposed Arabisms in the Old Testament," *JBL* 55 (1936) 106–7.

the first place, his view regarding the fundamental meaning of the Arabic root is erroneous. Its most basic sense appears to be related to the actions of spreading, disclosing or publishing. It can refer to anything from the disclosure of information to the spread of a disease.[15] The data to which Driver appeals for support are primarily found in only the fourth form of the Arabic verb and therefore his interpretation of the evidence does not adequately reflect the range and complexity of the root's semantic field.[16] Secondly, even in those places where the drinking of water is mentioned, the sense of greedy overindulgence which Driver stresses is not really apparent. The verb does imply the consumption of all the water, to be sure, but there is not the slightest indication that this is due to reasons of extravagance or intemperance.[17] It appears, therefore, that Driver has focused too exclusively on only a portion of the data contained under this Arabic root and has inexactly interpreted that which he has isolated.

2.1.4. ZWR, *al-zūr // zārîm*

The Hebrew word *zārîm* ("strangers, foreigners") appears a number of times in close proximity to the word *ʿārîṣîm* ("terrifying, awe-inspiring ones"). This collocation has caused Lothar Kopf to suggest that perhaps the first Hebrew word may in these instances carry the connotation of "violent, forceful ones." He notes the presence of the same meaning in the cognate Arabic root *zwr* to support his contention.[18]

[15] *Ṣiḥāḥ* 1. 447; *Lisān* 9. 454–55; *Qāmūs* 3. 25; *Maqāyīs* 2. 365.

[16] Part of Driver's difficulty may be due to the fact that, like some Arabic dictionaries, he sees two separate hollow roots here, one with a *yāʾ* as the middle radical and the other with a *wāw*. Within each of these he finds the meaning that is important for his argument – "to drink all the water found in a container." The sense mentioned above, "to spread, disclose, etc.," is found only in the form with a middle *yāʾ* according to this schema. Because it is found in both forms one can get the impression that the former meaning is more primary. Lane notes (990), however, that this division is a mistake and the form with the *yāʾ* is the true root. This is Lane's personal opinion, and it need not be the case. If he is correct, however, and the data are all collected within this one root it is apparent that overindulgence does not have the fundamental significance that Driver contends it does.

[17] It is quite possible that the same basic meaning "spreading around" is operative in those texts that speak of water. This is all the more likely since the drinking always occurs in the context of a group of people or animals. It could be that the action of passing the water around and making it available to all is the main focus of this verb. There appears to be a similar usage in the text from Abū Zaid which al-Azharī cites: "I left my wares in such and such a place and the people came and spread them (my wares) around (*aḏāʿūha*)." (*Tahḏīb* 3. 149)

[18] L. Kopf, "Arabische Etymologien und Parallelen zum Bibelwörterbuch," *VT* 8 (1958) 171–72.

Three factors work against this proposal and make it less persuasive than it at first appears. First of all, it is unnecessary from the semantic point of view. The Hebrew word translated in its usual way is not out of place and makes perfect sense. The presence of foreigners among the ruthless, violent ones (or, for that matter, identified with them) is not unreasonable (Isa 25:5, 29:5; Ezek 28:7, 31:12; Ps 54:5).[19] A second difficulty is encountered in the Arabic data Kopf relies upon. He mentions the expression *bizzūr* ("with force, forcibly") as an example of Arabic use of the root in a way that suggests violence. The fact that this is strictly an expression from modern Arabic weakens his position.[20] This is particularly damaging in that this is the only place where the sense of violence that is basic to Kopf's argument is clearly found. The common meaning of the older usage is simply one of strength with none of the fierceness Kopf highlights. A third shortcoming is the fact the meaning "strength," from the internal point of view, is one of the more trivial ones found under the root. It is only the nominal form cited above (*zūr*) that makes any reference to strength, and meanings related to this are not found in any of the verbal forms. "To visit," "to lie, deceive," and "to incline" appear to be the major groupings under which practically all words fall. Given these deficiencies, Kopf's argument is not "forceful."[21]

[19] It should be noted that in some cases the variant reading *zēdîm* ("insolent ones") is proposed in an effort to improve the sense. This is usually based upon evidence from the versions.

[20] Those listing it as a modern form include H. Wehr, *A Dictionary of Modern Written Arabic* (Ithaca: Spoken Language Services, 1976) 386; J. G. Hava, *Arabic-English Dictionary* (Beirut: Catholic Press, 1951) 301; and R. P. A. Dozy, *Supplément aux Dictionnaries Arabes* (Leiden: E. J. Brill, 1881) 1. 612, who cites primarily modern sources for the meaning. Exactly how this sense of "force" became part of the Arabic meaning is a disputed point. Reference is made below to the common notion of a Persian provenance for the sense. Others suggest different possibilities. For example, A. Wahrmund, *Handwörterbuch der neu-arabischen und deutschen Sprache* (Giessen: J. Ricker'sche Verlags-Buchhandlung, 1898) 1. 856 believes it may be a phonetic corruption from *jaur* ("injustice, oppression, tyranny").

[21] See the *Maqāyīs* 3. 36–37 for a discussion of the primary meanings of the root. A further question mark is added by reference to Lane (1269), who inquires about the legitimacy of the meaning "strength" because it is also found in the Persian form of the word. If it is an arabicized borrowing from Persian, any discussion of the light the Arabic data can shed on the Hebrew word is pointless. The fact noted above that this meaning is not found elsewhere within the root is a point in favor of external origin. The parallel with Persian is discussed in the Arabic dictionaries. The *Jamhara* (2. 327) says "they claim it is Persian since *al-zūr* in Persian means strength." Al-Azharī (13. 242) also points out the "agreement" between Arabic and Persian. The *Tāj*, however, is not so sure it is a borrowed form (3. 246). Regardless of the origin of this particular expression, it should be observed that other meanings of the word which are listed by Lane ("judgement, intelligence, deliciousness") have been completely left out of the discussion by Kopf.

2.1.5. ĠWṮ, *al-ġawīṯ* // *ʿûšû*

The word *ʿûšû* in Joel 4:11 is a *hapax* and Wilhelm Rudolph has proposed this Arabic word as a cognate and given it the meaning "haste."[22] But the support for this translation of the Arabic word is not altogether convincing. Lane does list "vehemence in running," which is found in two of the Arabic sources, as a possible meaning, but better attested and more widely present are meanings which expresses a sense of aiding or helping another.[23] This latter sense is particularly strong in light of the fact that none of the other nominal or verbal forms of the root suggest haste.[24] Rudolph has offered a proposal that is based on an extremely secondary and rare meaning for the Arabic root. In Joel 4:11, in all probablility, there is a call to the nations to come and help, not to come quickly. Rudolph dismisses the former possibility by maintaining that the verb would then have to be in the *hitpael* conjugation. Yet this is not necessarily so since neither the context nor the syntax demands a reflexive form of the verb.[25] The sentence may then perhaps best be read "Help, and come, all you surrounding nations!"[26]

2.1.6. QṬB, *al-quṭ(u)b* // *qeṭeb*

The word *qeṭeb* of Deut 32:24 is usually translated as "destruction" or "scourge" based on its use elsewhere (Ps 91:6; Hos 13:14; Isa 28:2), but Baruch Margalit has proposed the reading "spots" and offers this Arabic word as sup-

[22] W. Rudolph, "Ein Beitrag zum hebräischen Lexikon aud dem Joelbuch," in *Hebräische Wortforschung* (VTSup 16; Leiden: E.J. Brill, 1967) 249.

[23] *Maqāyīs* 4. 400; Lane, 2306. Lane lists the *Qāmūs* (1. 177) and the *ʿUbāb* of al-Ṣaġānī as the two sources containing this meaning. Others that do not have it include the *Tahḏīb* (8. 176–77) and the *Tāj* (1. 636).

[24] One could argue that the primary meaning of giving aid or coming to the assistance of another implicitly contains a notion of haste. This is an assumption and reads too much into the evidence. If this were the case, one would expect to find at least a hint of the sense of urgency in the Arabic sources, but there is none to be found.

[25] Rudolph later changed his opinion on this word and went with the translation "help" based on the same Arabic word. See his *Joel – Amos – Obadja – Jona* (Gütersloh: Mohn, 1971) 77.

[26] A number of English versions, including *NJB* and *NAB*, do opt for the translation "haste," but this is for another reason entirely. They base this on a textual emendation and read *hûšû* for *ʿûšû*. This is one of the proposed alternatives in *BHS*. A further difficulty with this proposal that needs to be recognized is the fact that each of the three consonants of the Hebrew root can have two counterparts in Arabic. This, together with the internal Arabic problem regarding whether or not the two roots with a medial *wāw* and *yāʾ* are related, raises serious questions about Rudolph's proposal.

port.[27] The first question to ask concerns how Margalit is able to make the leap from "thorns" to "spots," which he then relates to the effects of plague. The connection is not an obvious one and he does not offer any explanation. There are also some difficulties regarding the Arabic evidence. According to Lane, any meaning having to do with thorns is secondary and not very well attested.[28] Only two sources are relevant. The first is from Abū Ḥanīfa of the late third century of the Islamic era who wrote a book on plants. He claims the word *quṭb* refers to a type of plant that grows along the ground and has a thorny blossom that is painful to walk upon. The second source is al-Liḥyanī who is a bit earlier and says it is a species of thorn from which three thorns emerge.[29] Beyond these few references, none of which is from a source that may be deemed primary or authoritative, there is no mention of thorns. The chief meaning of the word appears rather to be "axis" or "pivot."[30] It therefore seems that Margalit has isolated this one rare meaning of the word and given it an importance greater than the evidence allows.

2) Reliance Upon a Single Source

2.2.1. BṬḤ I, *baṭaḥa, yabṭaḥu // bôṭēaḥ*

G. R. Driver, basing his proposal on this Arabic root, gives the sense "tumble down" to the word *bôṭēaḥ* in Jer 12:5.[31] The full significance of the sentence then, according to him, is that if one is tumbling and falling in the safe country one cannot hope to survive in the overgrown and difficult area of the Jordan valley. Driver appears to be reading too much into this Arabic root. The first meaning he quotes for it, "to lay face down," is well attested and is clearly connected to the other primary sense the root has of spreading out or extending along the ground.[32] However, an important thing to note with regard to this meaning is that in every case where lying on the ground is mentioned there is

[27] B. Margalit, "Ugaritic Contributions to Hebrew Lexicography," *ZAW* 99 (1987) 392.

[28] Lane, 2541–42. As noted earlier, one must be very careful when using Lane's lexicon beginning with the root *qadda*. This is particularly true for those entries which are not found in the main body of the work and refer the user to the supplement. The root *qaṭaba* appears to be well treated and amply documented. Nonetheless, caution must be exercised in these later volumes.

[29] Both of these sources are mentioned in the *Lisān* (2. 176) and the *Tāj* (1. 433). Al-Azharī also mentions a quotation from Laith in which it is defined as a plant with thorns (*Tahḏīb* 9. 3) but Lane makes no reference to this source.

[30] *Maqāyīs* 5. 105.

[31] G. R. Driver, "Linguistic and Textual Problems: Jeremiah," *JQR* 28 (1937–38) 111–12.

[32] Lane, 216; *Maqāyīs* 1. 260–61 gives the basic meaning as "spreading, stretching."

an element of intention involved: either the person has willfully chosen to do so or is thrown down by another. There is no sense of the clumsy or dangerous free-fall that Driver's definition "tumble down" implies. The Arabic sources are quite clear that the word does not refer to a stumble or a trip but the simple act of stretching or extending out along the ground.[33] It is apparent that Driver is guilty of relying upon a single dictionary to give the Hebrew word the sense he seeks. He has taken the meaning "tumble down" which is found in only one inauthoritative source and has constructed his argument on this unstable foundation.[34]

2.2.2. TNN, *al-tīnān // tannîm*

Isa 13:21-22 describes the disaster that will befall Babylon by enumerating a list of different animals that will overrun the region and inhabit the dwelling places of the people. The last animals mentioned are the *tannîm*, a word well attested in the biblical literature that is usually translated as "jackal" (Jer 9:10; Ps 44:20; Lam 4:3). G. R. Driver claims that a more proper translation of the word is "wolf" based upon the Arabic *tīnān*.[35] This is another example of isolation of one meaning that is not well established in the sources. It is found in the *Qāmūs*,[36] but attributed to one single poetic source, al-Aḵṭal.[37] Because it is not found elsewhere, this particular meaning should not be given too much weight.[38] A meaning that is much better supported by the evidence and is con-

[33] *Lisān* 3. 236–37; *Qāmūs* 1. 223–24; *Tāj* 2. 124–25.

[34] The source he uses for "tumble down" is Hava's *Arabic-English Dictionary* (37) which he misquotes. The form in Hava with this meaning is not the fourth (*ʾabṭaḥa*), as Driver claims, but the seventh (*inbaṭaḥa*). The fact that this meaning is not found in any other dictionary seriously questions its reliability. Driver seems to be aware of the intentional aspect of this verb when, in pointing out the semantic connection with the Hebrew cognate, he observes that to throw oneself down before another is to seek protection and therefore is an act of trust. He must consequently rely upon the poorly attested other meaning of "tumble down" to defend his position. The problems involved with relying solely upon Hava for Arabic data will be given fuller treatment in the next chapter.

[35] G. R. Driver, "Birds in the Old Testament II. Birds in Life," *PEQ* 87 (1955) 135, n. 4.

[36] *Qāmūs* 4, 207; the *Lisān* also contains the word, saying that al-Aḵṭal was the only one to use it (16. 224–25).

[37] The *Jamhara* (2. 31) suggests that the word is not universally used among the Arabs with the remark "The wolf is called the *tīnān* in some languages (dialects), and al-Aḵṭal uses it in his poetry."

[38] *Tahḏīb* 14. 254; *Tāj* 9. 153–54; Lane, 318. See also *BDB* (1072), which mentions the Arabic meaning "jackal" but considers it "rare." The questionable nature of this meaning is also seen in the fact that neither Freytag nor Hava, who normally rely a great deal upon the *Qāmūs*, have included it in their works.

tained in all lexicons is that of "great serpent, dragon" (*tinnīn*). If Driver were to insist upon arguing for a meaning based upon the Arabic sources he would be on much more secure ground were he to opt for this meaning.[39] A shortcoming is that it would not fit the context as well as "wolf" does. It therefore appears best to give the word its conventional Hebrew sense and see it as a reference to jackals.[40]

2.2.3. ḤFŠ II, *ḥaffaša, yuḥaffišu // ḥopšît*

In an attempt to clarify the problematic word *ḥopšît* (2 Kgs 15:5//2 Chr 26:21), Alfred Guillaume proposes the translation "he dwelt in his house without leaving it" based on the Arabic verb cited above, to which he assigns the meaning "to stay in one's tent."[41] He believes this fits perfectly in the context since the king has been stricken with leprosy and is forced to live in exile. But the tenuousness of the argument can be grasped by recognizing how poorly attested this meaning is for *ḥaffaša*. The only dictionary which clearly has the definition Guillaume has proposed for this verbal form is that of Hava. None of the primary sources offers this meaning. In fact, Lane does not list a verbal form at all and simply has nominal forms, among which is one he defines as "a small tent."[42] Beyond this, the sense of permanence and isolation on the part

[39] This is, in fact, the translation given in the *KJV*. A shortcoming of this suggestion is the fact that the Hebrew word is a plural form while the Arabic is singular, which is not a major obstacle but does complicate the issue. On top of this is the question of the origin of the Arabic word. *Tinnīn* could be from some other ancient language, and we may have a case here where it might be more appropriate to inquire what Hebrew can tell us about the Arabic form rather than vice versa.

[40] This suggestion is further supported by the structure of the verse. The word is parallel to *ʾiyyîm* in the first part of the verse. These two words share the meaning "jackal." Note that the two also appear in close proximity in Isa 34:13–14, the only other time *ʾiyyîm* is found in Isaiah. The word is found under the heading *tn* in *HALAT* (1619), which says the derivation is unknown but clearly gives it the meaning "jackal."

[41] Alfred Guillaume, *Hebrew and Arabic Lexicography IV* (Leiden: E. J. Brill, 1965) 6. Originally published in *Abr-Nahrain* 4 (1963–64) 1–18.

[42] Hava, 132; Lane, 601; *Maqāyīs* 2. 86. Of course, this is not a major problem since the existence of the nominal form meaning "a small tent" would make the meaning ("to dwell in a small tent") of a verbal form immediately clear, given the proper context. There is a lack of agreement among the major dictionaries on how to treat and define this root. The *Ṣiḥāḥ* includes meanings having to do with hard rain and the running of horses (1. 279). On the other hand, the *Lisān* (8. 175) does define it as "to reside in a tent," but it does not suggest that this is a permanent residence as Guillaume insists. The *Tāj* does not have this meaning at all, which is unusual given its comprehensive character (5. 299–300). Most curious is the meaning given in the *Jamhara*, which

of the tent dweller that is such an important part of Guillaume's argument is lacking in the sources, including Hava's.[43] To construct a case on such incomplete evidence is an unsound approach and suggests that Guillaume has not followed his own advice to "follow the path of comparative philology and common sense."[44]

2.2.4. ḤLʾ I, *ḥalaʾa, yaḥlaʾu* // *ḥelʾâ*

In an obvious case of isolating a very rare and secondary Arabic meaning Guillaume has linked this Arabic word, which he translates "to rub rust off a mirror," with Hebrew *ḥelʾâ* ("rust").[45] One of the basic meanings of the Arabic word is that of rubbing two stones together to produce a powder to be placed on the eyes for medicinal purposes.[46] Guillaume's meaning seems to come from an elaboration of this meaning put forth by one of the Arabic sources, that of Ibn al-Sikkīt (ninth century C.E.), who adds the further step of using the powder to rub off the rust of a mirror before applying it to the eyes.[47] Beyond this reference, there is no other mention of rust under this root.[48]

---

claims it describes a person squinting through the eyelashes by knitting the eyebrows together (1. 158). Wahrmund (1. 526) gives a good sense of the wide range of meanings found within this root. It only lists meanings in the first form and includes such diverse senses as "to gather, peel, extract, chase away," and "to rain, do a favor, be destroyed by an ulcer" when vocalized with a *kasra*.

43 Certain definitions suggest that the exact opposite sense is a proper one. Some dictionaries contain a meaning that has to do with people congregating and meeting. The *Tāj* (5. 300), for example, says a *ḥafš* is a "meeting of people."

44 A further difficulty with Guillaume's proposal is the problematic nature of the phonemic equivalence he suggests. The Hebrew lettter *š* typically corresponds to Arabic *sīn* or *ṯāʾ*, but never to *šīn* as it must here. In its treatment of the root *HALAT* (328) observes that Guillaume's proposal goes against the usual sense of "freedom" that is basic to the Hebrew root. However, Guillaume's suggestion is not mentioned in the discussion of the word in 2 Kgs 15 in *HALAT*.

45 Guillaume, *Hebrew and Arabic Lexicography II*, 14. Originally published in *Abr Nahrain* 2 (1960–61) 5–35.

46 It can also refer to shaving or rubbing the skin. See *Ṣiḥāḥ* 1. 287; *Jamhara* 3. 135; *Tahḏīb* 5. 237–38; *Lisān* 1. 52–54; *Tāj* 1. 57–58.

47 See Lane, 622–23. The usual verb related to rust in Arabic is *ṣadaʾa*, which does carry the meaning of polishing a mirror by removing the rust from it. This word is found in the citation from Ibn al-Sikkīt, which further underlines the fact that the root *ḥalaʾa* is not to be identified with rust, contrary to Guillaume.

48 *HALAT* (302) has inaccurately cited Guillaume's proposal by listing it as the Arabic verb *ḥaliʾa* and assigning it the meaning "to rust." Note that there is also an error in *HALAT* regarding the page number of Guilluame's suggestion.

2.2.5. RṮD I, *raṯada, yarṯadu // yirpad*

Guillaume uses this Arabic form in an attempt to shed light on the verb *yirpad* in Job 41:22 and gives it the meaning "muddy."[49] Besides the obviously questionable nature of the equivalence on linguistic grounds, since Arabic *ṯāʾ* cannot be equated with Hebrew *p*, there exists some serious doubt regarding the dependability of the meaning. According to Lane, it is found only in the Turkish translation of the *Qāmūs*.[50] None of the standard dictionaries, including the *Qāmūs* in its original Arabic edition, carry the meaning.[51] This is therefore obviously an example of dependence upon one unreliable source.

2.2.6. SLM II, *al-taslīmī // šālēm*

In the course of a discussion on the many different uses of the root *šālēm* in the Song of Songs, H. Hirschberg offers this Arabic word and the meaning "consummation gift" as the key to unlocking the mystery of certain texts.[52] He observes that this word, which refers to the gift the bridegroom offers to the bride after consummation, fits the context nicely in view of the fact that one of the basic meanings of the Hebrew verb is "perfecting" or "concluding."

This proposal is highly suspect on two counts. First of all, the Arabic verb *salima* does not carry the sense of perfecting or concluding in any of its derived forms. This calls into question Hirschberg's contention that the word is somehow linked with the consummation component of "consummation gift." It is rather the giving of the groom to the bride that is being highlighted here, as an examination of the verb indicates. The word *taslīmī* is the verbal noun, or *maṣdar*, form of the verb in its second conjugation (*sallama*).[53] A primary meaning of this form of the verb is "to give or hand over to another person,"

[49] Guillaume, *Hebrew and Arabic Lexicography I*, 15. Originally published in *Abr-Nahrain* 1 (1959–60).

[50] Lane, 1031. In his preface (xxv–xxvi) Lane is highly critical of this work. Both Freytag and Hava also list the meaning which Guillaume puts forth. Lane notes that an overdependence upon the Turkish translation of the *Qāmūs*, often passing off its meanings as stemming from the original, is a hallmark of Freytag's work. The presence of the meaning in Hava can be attributed to his own heavy dependence on Freytag's lexicon.

[51] *Jamhara* 2. 37; *Tahḏīb* 14. 89; *Ṣiḥāḥ* 1. 465; *Lisān* 4. 151–52; *Qāmūs* 1. 304; *Maqāyīs* 2. 487. It should be pointed out, however, that the *Tāj* (2. 350) mentions that al-Ṣaġānī's dictionary contains the meaning "cloudiness."

[52] H. Hirschberg, "Some Additional Arabic Etymologies in Old Testament Lexicography," *VT* 11 (1961) 380.

[53] Properly speaking, *taslīm* is the verbal noun form. The final *ī*, which is found in Hirschberg's article, makes the word adjectival.

which suggests that it is the transfer of the gift from the groom to the bride that is the key moment the word is concerned with and not the action that preceded it.[54] A second shortcoming of Hirschberg's proposition is equally damaging: the Arabic word he bases his argument on is so obscure that it is not found in any of the basic dictionaries. He is well aware of this fact since he notes that this is a practice that is customary "among certain Arabic tribes," and he cites a German volume on Egyptian folklore as his only source for this information.[55] Using Arabic data that is so dubious to defend one's argument is highly questionable and ill-advised.

2.2.7. ḌBʾ I, *ḍabaʾa, yaḍbaʾu // ṣābāʾ*

Kopf has tentatively put forth this verb, which be translates "to assemble," as one that can be useful to interpret the Hebrew root *ṣābāʾ*.[56] Once again, a meaning which is very uncertain has been enlisted to confirm a suggestion. The root does not carry this significance in any of the standard dictionaries. It is found in the *Al-Mukaṣṣaṣ* of Ibn Sīdaʾ, and Kopf cites this evidence, but he also admits that this definition is not supported by any literary references.[57] Putting forth such admittedly poor evidence in an attempt to shed light on the meaning of this Hebrew root is pointless.

2.2.8. ʿRḌ I, *ʿaruḍa, yaʿruḍu // taʿărôṣ*

In an effort to establish a parallel structure with *tirdôp* of the second colon in Job 13:25 G. R. Driver translates the word *taʿărôṣ* in the earlier part of the verse as "follow," enlisting this Arabic verb for support.[58] Hava is the only dictionary which contains this meaning; it is not found in any of the primary sources.[59] It appears, therefore, that the evidence upon which Driver's pro-

[54] *Ṣiḥāḥ* 1. 607–08; *Lisān* 15. 181–83; *Qāmūs* 4. 131–33; Lane, 1412–13.

[55] H. A. Winkler, *Ägyptische Volkskunde*, 209–10. Hirschberg gives none of the bibliographical data on this source.

[56] Kopf, 196. This proposal is cited in *HALAT* (933) despite its questionable nature.

[57] The meaning "assemble" is not found in any of the basic works. The primary meaning they contain is that of hiding, concealing or clinging. See *Jamhara* 3. 207; *Ṣiḥāḥ* 2. 4; *Lisān* 1. 105–06; *Qāmūs* 1. 21; *Tāj* 1. 88–89; *Maqāyīs* 3. 389. It is particularly telling that the *Tāj*, which is heavily indebted to the works of Ibn Sīdaʾ, does not list this meaning.

[58] G. R. Driver, "Problems in the Hebrew Text of Proverbs," *Bib* 32 (1951) 180, n 2.

[59] Hava, 464. See Lane, 2002–13, where the word "follow" does not appear once in the course of more than ten triple-columned pages which treat this root. Cf. *Tahḏīb* 1. 454–69; *Ṣiḥāḥ* 2.

posal is based comes from a single, inadequate lexical resource.[60] Rather than insisting upon seeing parallelism at work here, it seems better to simply accept the normal meaning of the Hebrew verb, "to cause to tremble." This highlights the tone of this verse in which Job is accusing God of wasting time: "Are you going to cause an already wind-blown leaf to tremble? Are you going to pursue dry straw?"[61]

3) Disregard for the Semantic Field

2.3.1. BNW/Y I, *banā, yabnī*// *ʾibbāneh*

The origin of the Hebrew word *ʾibbāneh* (Gen 16:2; 30:3) is not completely clear and it has been connected with both the roots *bn* and *bānāh*. Kopf has used the above Arabic verb, to which he gives the meaning "to beget a child," to argue for the latter alternative.[62] His chief support in this is the expression *banā ʿala ʾahlihi*, which describes the man's going in to his wife for sexual relations.[63] Kopf maintains that this suggests that the original meaning of the verb was "to beget." There are some problems with his thesis. First of all, Kopf does not demonstrate how or why this must necessarily be the original significance of the verb. He simply states that this is the case. It is tempting to connect the senses "beget" and "build," but impossible to prove. It appears, rather, that the development was probably from the meaning "to build" to that of "to consummate a marriage." The expression originated in the erection of the nuptial tent and came to be a common expression for the marriage ceremony characterized by the bride being led to the tent. Eventually, it came to be used to mean the consummation of the marriage. A careful examination of the Arabic data raises further doubts. If "beget" were indeed a fundamental part of this root's semantic field, we would expect to find some evidence of this within its vari-

---

98–102. Ibn Fāris, in his *Maqāyīs* (4. 269–81), argues that the various branches of this root's semantic configuration can be reduced to the meaning "to be wide."

[60] It is all the more disturbing, therefore, to see that Driver's suggestion has apparently been incorporated into the *NEB* which translates the word as "chase." The *REB*, a revision of the *NEB*, changes the translation to "harass."

[61] In the same way, Driver's reliance upon the same verb with different vocalization (*ʿariḍa*, "to be within sight of") is questionable. This is, in all probability, rooted in the well-attested meaning of "to show, expose, present, etc.," and so cannot be used as support for the meaning "to follow." This is particularly so since, as we have seen, this latter sense is not found in the root.

[62] Kopf, 168.

[63] This expression is found, for example, with Ibn al-Sikkīt as quoted by al-Azharī in the *Tahḏīb* 15. 493.

ous forms and permutations. But there is none to be found.[64] It appears that when the word is used in reference to relations between the sexes, it refers only to the act of intercourse with little regard for its possible consequences. There is, as noted above, some indication in the sources that the reference is even more specific and focuses upon the consummation of a marriage. This is seen both in the verbal form, which some sources say speaks of the man's going in to his wife for the first time, and the nominal form *bānin*, which can mean "bridegroom." There is in the end, then, no real Arabic evidence to buttress Kopf's claim. He has focused upon this one narrow meaning and divorced it from the wider context of the Arabic root's semantic field.

2.3.2. JLD I, *jalada, yajlidu // geled*

In the course of a discussion in which Hirschberg points out that some Semitic roots combine the notions of "skin" and "carnal knowledge," he mentions the Arabic verb *jalada*, which he translates "to deflower, rape," as one which exhibits this feature.[65] He says this Arabic root and the Hebrew *geled* share the meaning "skin" and, while a reference to carnal knowledge is not found in the Hebrew form, such a sense clearly exists in the Arabic.

In general, Hirschberg is correct in his observation. There is ample evidence among both nominal and verbal forms that "skin" is an important part of the Arabic root's semantic range. In the same way, one of the possible meanings of the basic verbal conjugation is "to lie with a woman or female slave."[66] However, there is a difficulty in the way Hirschberg interprets this latter meaning. By adding to it the sense of rape and violation, he gives it a coercive and violent tone that is not found in the Arabic sources. Perhaps he has been influenced in this by some of the other attested meanings of the root which can carry a more forceful sense including "to hit or hurt the skin," "to whip," and "to contend with in a fight." Nothing of this violent notion, however, can be discerned in the meanings connected to sexual relations.[67] It appears, therefore, that

[64] In fact, one verbal form seems to be directly opposed to the presence of "beget" in the root. The fifth conjugation, *tabannā*, can mean "to adopt a child as one's own." It is denominative from "son," and does not derive from the first form. The treatment of the expression *banā ʿala ahlihi* found in the *Tāj* (10. 47) is particulary insightful since it highlights the problems in its interpretation throughout history in light of related material in the *hadīth*. This clearly indicates that the meaning of the expression is not as well established as Kopf contends. See also *Qāmūs* 4. 307; Lane, 260–63; *Maqāyīs* 1. 302–3.

[65] Hirschberg, 373–74.

[66] *Qāmūs* 1. 293–94; *Tāj* 2. 321–23; *Maqāyīs* 1. 471; Lane, 442–43.

[67] There is a further meaning related to carnal knowledge that Hirschberg has not mentioned.

Hirschberg has read this violent sense into the Arabic root through his insufficient attention to its semantic range.

2.3.3. JYŠ, *al-jayš* // *hāmôn*

Kopf has suggested that the Arabic word *jayš* exhibits the same semantic development as he discerns for the Hebrew word *hāmôn:* from sound (*Geräusch*) and noise (*Lärm*) to raging crowd (*wogende Menge*) and army (*Heer*).[68] This is a false statement. Nothing in the Arabic sources indicates that "noise" or "din" was ever a part of this root's semantic range. The primary sense of the root appears to be that of agitation or overflowing. The root can refer, among other things, to a pot, the sea, an animal, one's soul or one's stomach.[69] It does also carry the well-attested meaning of "army," but, contrary to Kopf, this has not developed from other meanings related to sound.[70]

2.3.4. ḴLQ I, *ḵaliqa, yaḵluqu* // *ḥēleq*

To support his translation of the words *ḥelqām baḥayyîm* (Ps 17:14) as "destroy them in the midst of life," G. R. Driver calls upon this Arabic verb which he indicates has the meaning "to be shabby, worn out."[71] This meaning

---

Lane remarks that the verb can also be used in reference to the act of masturbation. He gives a series of terms to which the word is related including the graphically euphemistic *nakaḥa al-yad* – "to marry the hand." This connotation, of course, cannot be used to support Hirschberg's inclusion of violence and force in the meaning.

[68] L. Kopf, "Arabische Etymologien und Parallelen zum Bibelwörterbuch," *VT* 9 (1959) 254.

[69] *Jamhara* 2. 98; *Ṣiḥāḥ* 1. 226; *Lisān* 8. 164–65; *Tāj* 4. 291–92; *Maqāyīs* 1. 499; Lane, 493–94. Since the word can refer to agitation of the stomach or soul it is not surprising to find "fear" as a possible meaning. A text from al-Aḥmar is quoted by al-Azharī which contains the notions of fear and noise side by side: "Agitation (fear), scraping sounds and noise departed from the night." (*Tahḏīb* 11. 135) It is possible that this type of collocation may have led Kopf to conclude that the word used for "fear" (*jayš*) was a synonym for "scraping sounds" and "noise" and this was the basis of his definition. However, there is nothing in the syntax of the sentence that demands such an identification and, as has been mentioned above, there is no data in the Arabic sources to sustain this view.

[70] The only dictionary to include a meaning in support of Kopf's contention is Hava (108) who translates the word "shriek, voice" along with the more usual "army." However, he notes this is only found in the modern dialect of Syria. This turns Kopf's theory completely upside-down. Instead of a development from "sound" to "army," the modern Arabic data suggest the movement was in the opposite direction. It is interesting to note that in its treatment of this word *HALAT* (240) refers to Kopf's proposal but is selective in its citation. It mentions his suggestion of a development from "crowd" (*Menge*) to "army" (*Heer*), but says nothing about these meanings developing from others connected to sound and noise.

[71] G. R. Driver, "Notes on the Psalms I. 1–72.," *JTS* 43 (1942) 152.

is well attested in the sources and often refers to a garment or cloak that is smooth and, therefore, old and in poor condition. It can further be used when referring to a person whose face is worn and whose youth has departed.[72]

Driver's choice of this Arabic verb to support his argument is an unusual one. The connection between sudden, external destruction in the midst of life and natural wear and tear after many years is neither clear nor obvious. The proposal becomes particularly problematic in view of the larger context of the root. The chief meaning of the verb when vocalized differently as *k̲alaqa* is "to measure" and "to create."[73] The latter form is closely identified with divine creation and the act of bringing into existence out of nothingness. Indeed, in the *Qurʾān* Allah is the sole subject of the verb. This gives the word the exact opposite meaning to the sense which Driver posits.[74] Arabic is notorious as a language in which contradictory meanings of the same word live comfortably side by side, but the lack of any reference to destruction in the dictionaries argues against Driver's interpretation and suggests he has ignored the verb's semantic context.[75]

2.3.5. ZQQ, *al-ziqq // yāzōqqû*

Marvin Pope, in treating the word *yāzōqqû* (Job 28:1), seeks support for his contention that it refers to the process of refining gold by citing this Arabic word as applied "especially" to the bellows of the forge.[76] This is rather misleading. The word means simply a receptacle or sack, in particular one made of skin.[77] To claim that it is chiefly identified with a bellows is to go beyond the

72 These meanings may be related to that of becoming smooth, in the sense of worn, which is well attested in the sources. Note al-Laith's quotation cited in *Tahd̲īb* 7. 29: "The *ʾak̲laq* is the smoothest of every thing." See also *Ṣiḥāḥ* 1. 366–67; *Lisān* 11. 372–74; *Qāmūs* 3. 236–37; *Tāj* 6. 335–37; *Maqāyīs* 2. 213–14.

73 Lane, 799–800.

74 The meaning, of course, belongs to the formal discourse of Muslim theology and is secondary with respect to the semantic bases of the consonantal root.

75 The treatment of the root in *HALAT* (310) seems to support this view. The Arabic meaning "to be worn out" is cited, but there is no suggestion that it can be extended to convey the sense of destruction. Evidence from cognate sources like Ugaritic, Akkadian and Ethiopic is also noted, and in these languages the meaning "to die" is found.

76 M. Pope, *Job* (AB 15; Garden City, NY: Doubleday, 1965) 177–78.

77 This is in line with the meaning of skinning an animal, which is a major part of the root's semantic field, especially in the second verbal form. See, for example, *Tahd̲īb* 8. 262; *Ṣiḥāḥ* 1. 539; *Lisān* 12. 8–9; *Qāmūs* 3. 249; *Tāj* 6. 371–72; *Maqāyīs* 3. 4.

evidence of the primary Arabic sources which make no such specific reference.[78]

2.3.6. ṬRF I, *ṭarafa, yaṭrifu* // *ṭerep*

The Hebrew word *ṭerep* can mean both "prey" (Gen 49:9; Amos 3:4) and "food" (Mal 3:10; Job 24:5). The semantic development from "prey" and from the Hebrew root's basic meaning of "to tear or pluck" to "food" appears to be a logical and obvious one. But Philip J. Calderone believes the etymology is "obscure" and so he offers this Arabic verb, to which he gives the meaning "freshly picked," to help explain the presence of the meaning "food."[79] By doing so he has both carelessly misread the Arabic data and given it a distorted interpretation.

The first point to be noted is that the meaning "freshly picked" is not found in any of the sources. Not surprisingly, therefore, Calderone does not give the source of this meaning. He has probably reworked some of the more established senses of the word to suit his needs and defend his position. The impression this creates, that the root *ṭrf* is related to food, cannot be sustained by the evidence. One single meaning of an Arabic root has been falsely identified and then isolated from other meanings (many of which are more basic) thereby painting an inaccurate picture of the semantic shape and contours of the Arabic comparison.

The most fundamental meanings of words related to this Arabic root appear to fall under three headings. The first type are those that have to do with sight and vision. Many of the verbal forms in the first conjugation refer to looking and a number of nominal forms have to do with the eye and parts of the eye. A second type describes the end, extremity or side of an object. The third group has to do with the acquisition of something new or novel which one did not have before.[80] As mentioned above, there is no direct mention in the sources of Calderone's meaning or any reference to food, but he has probably based his argument on data which are contained in the first and third of these three categories.

[78] Although a connection with bellows is not found in Lane (1238) or the other dictionaries, a few verbal forms call to mind the sense of blowing that he mentions. One speaks of a bird's ejecting food from its bill into the mouth of its young. Hava does have the meaning "bellows of a hammersmith" for the phrase *ziqq al-ḥaddād* (291), but its absence elsewhere warns against giving the meaning the importance Pope attaches to it.

[79] P. J. Calderone, "*ḤDL*-II in Poetic Texts," *CBQ* 23 (1961) 453–54.

[80] *Ṣiḥāḥ* 2. 35–36; *Lisān* 11. 116–18; Lane, 1841–46.

One of the possible meanings of the first form of the verb describes a camel who does not feed on one pasturage but continually wanders from one area to another, tasting and feeding as it goes. This sense is also reflected in the noun *ṭarif* which refers to a camel that does not keep to one pasturage but constantly moves about.[81] It is important to note that the essential point in these words is the movement and fickleness of the animal, not the fact of eating. This becomes clear when we see that the same forms can be used to also refer to human beings who are not able to stay with the same spouse or companion but must always choose new partners.[82] The connection with the act of looking is apparent here and summed up succinctly in the common English proverb, "The grass is always greener on the other side."

The other area from which Calderone has probably drawn is those words which stress the newness or novelty of an object. These are also semantically linked with words for vision and sight, and can refer to anything that is new, recent, fresh, or pleasing. Although food can be their referent it is again clear that it is the action of seeing the physical form that is primary. The fact that it is food is coincidental and insignificant in determining the meaning of the word. We see this in the word *ṭarīf* used to describe fruit or the like with reference to color or pleasing shape.[83] It appears that Calderone's meaning "freshly picked" combines elements of both words which refer to grazing animals and words which highlight newness and freshness. Taken by themselves in isolation from the larger context of the semantic range of the root, these words appear to support his contention. But when we recognize that they are actually referring principally to vision and perception it must be admitted that any connection to food is purely secondary.

2.3.7. ᶜḎR I, *ᶜaḏara, yaᶜḏiru // ᶜăzārâ*

In his treatment of the word *ᶜăzārâ* (Ezek 43:14, 17), which he translates "surrounding ledge," G. R. Driver states that its root means "to protect or screen" and enlists this Arabic root for support.[84] He refers to a number of derived forms which he attempts to link with this proposed basic meaning including *ᶜaḏara* (*sic!*) ("virgin") as one who needs protection or screening,

[81] Lane, 1844.

[82] The *Tahḏīb* contains numerous texts giving the word this meaning. See, for example the quotation from Abū ᶜUbaida which defines it as a "woman who does not stay with one partner." (13. 319)

[83] Lane, 1845.

[84] G. R. Driver, "Ezechiel: Linguistic and Textual Evidence," *Bib* 35 (1954) 307–8.

ʿaḏīrun ("scar") as the covering of a wound, and the verbal form *ʿaḏara* ("to excuse") as denoting the protection or screening of persons. This is not an accurate interpretation of the Arabic data. The sense of screening is not a significant part of this root as a whole, and it is only his interpretation of the third of the three words mentioned above that can be plausibly defended. The meaning "to excuse" is a primary one for the root and while there may be said to be a conceivable connection between this and protecting a person, this connection is not explicitly made in the dictionaries. Regarding other verbal meanings, several, like "to beat someone" and "to flee," appear to contradict the sense of screening.[85]

Driver's analysis of the word *ʿaḏara* (actually *ʿaḏrāʾ*) is faulty and he misinterprets its semantic background. It does principally mean "virgin" but this is not due to the need to protect the young woman as Driver contends. One of the other meanings of the verb is "to cut" or "to circumcise," and this is the semantic context within which we should situate the word "virgin." This becomes clear when we note the related term *ʿuḏrah* ("hymen"). What makes a female a virgin is that which will be cut or rent during sexual intercourse. The word also can mean "the loss of one's (a female's) virginity," which clearly points up that it is the act of breaking or cutting the hymen that is the focus of the word. Furthermore, the same word can also denote the act of circumcision or the foreskin which will be cut off in that operation.[86] This also highlights the error in Driver's interpretation of "scar" as the covering of a wound. It is perhaps more accurate to relate it to the sense of cutting that is mentioned above. Driver has clearly been too narrow in his interpretation of the semantic range of the Arabic root and has consequently overlooked some primary meanings which challenge his proposal.[87]

2.3.8. ʿW/YQ II, *ʿawwaqa, yuʿawwiqu // ʿāqat*

Since the word *ʿāqat* in Ps 55:4 cannot be related to any known Hebrew root, it is alternately viewed as a textual corruption or an Aramaism.[88] G. R.

[85] *Tahḏīb* 2. 306–10; *Lisān* 6. 219–21; *Qāmūs* 2. 88–89.

[86] Driver does mention this word but only says it means "foreskin" and then, in an effort to strengthen his case, suggests that this is due to fact that it is a protective covering. Lane (1985) connects it more directly with circumcision and this is clearly seen in the meaning from the *Tāj*: "the portion of skin which the circumciser cuts off."

[87] The *Maqāyīs* (4. 253–57) gives a clear and succinct summary of the wide range of meanings found in this root but none of them have anything to do with protection.

[88] *BDB* lists it as an Aramaic form and includes it under the root עוק (734).

Driver believes the MT form is sound and clarifies it by way of the Arabic hollow verbs *ʿawwaqa* and *ʿayyaqa*, which he translates as "squealed" and "vociferated," respectively.[89] He then gives the Hebrew word the meaning "cry of glee." Regarding the first Arabic verb he cites, this meaning is not found in any of the standard dictionaries. The only data remotely related to Driver's sense are two nominal forms meaning "the cry of the crow" and "a sound that issues from the belly of a beast when it is going along."[90] Dozy does contain the verb, and Driver has identified this as his source. However, Dozy has "to mew" (*miauler*), not "squeal" or "vociferate" as his meaning.[91]

There is a further, more serious, problem with Driver's use of Dozy. The two sources Dozy lists for his meaning "to mew" are both from dictionaries of modern colloquial Arabic. The evidence is therefore of little or no value in treating the biblical material.[92] The situation regarding Driver's second verb is more promising but still problematic. It is found with the meaning "vociferated," which supports Driver's contention.[93] However, there is not the slightest hint in any of the sources of the element of glee which Driver posits. In fact, contrary to Driver, in the *Tāj* it carries the meaning "sound of rebuke." It appears, then, that he has amplified and adapted the data to prove his point.[94]

2.3.9. QḌY III, *qāḍā, yuqāḍī // nĕqîṣennâ*

The word *nĕqîṣennâ* in Isa 7:6 has caused some difficulties in interpretation and G. R. Driver has offered this Arabic verb, which he translates "to negotiate, bargain with," as a cognate parallel in order to give the sentence the following sense: "Let us negotiate with it (Judah), then let us detach it and win it over to ourselves."[95]

[89] G. R. Driver, "Supposed Arabisms," 111.

[90] *Jamhara* 3. 134; *Ṣiḥāḥ* 2. 176–77; *Qāmūs* 3. 279; Lane, 2199. The two forms are *ʿāq* and *ʿuwāq*. The primary meanings connected to this Arabic root are concerned with notions of hindering and preventing.

[91] Dozy, 2. 190. It should be noted that Dozy includes this meaning at the end of his entry, after he has listed the more usual definitions found elsewhere. He also has Driver's other verb, *ʿayyaqa*, with the exact same meaning (195).

[92] This characteristic of Dozy's dictionary and the danger of relying too heavily upon it will be given a more in-depth treatment in the next chapter.

[93] *Tāj* 12. 104; Lane, 2212.

[94] For a similar treatment of the problems surrounding this word and the need to clearly delineate the two roots involved see H.-P. Müller, "Die Wurzeln עיק, יעק, und עוק," *VT* 21 (1971) 556–59.

[95] Driver, "Isaiah I–XXXIX," 29.

Whether or not Driver's suggestion fits the passage in Isaiah, a basic obstacle the proposal encounters is the lack of support for it in the Arabic dictionaries. The primary meaning of the Arabic root *qḍy* is "to finalize, bring to an end, deal with, pass (time or judgement)," and from this come the nominal forms *qāḍī* ("judge") and *qaḍīya* ("case in court"). The verbal form *qāḍā* ("to raise a case against someone, to sue") is based on these forms. Consequently, there developed a very clear presence of the theme of judging within the root. There is no evidence of Driver's meaning "negotiate" in the sources.[96] In other words, the accent is not on the action of two individuals in resolving differences between them, but on the mediating role of the judge in deciding the issue. This is clear when we note the translation given for the third form of the verb (*qāḍa*), which Driver has cited: it is typically rendered "to summon someone before a judge."[97] To properly base his argument on this Arabic data, then, Driver would first have to establish that there was a judge involved in the negotiations between the Judahites and Arameans/Israelites.[98] As his proposal stands, Driver has totally ignored the evidence which a wider examination of the root's semantic field uncovers.

[96] Other meanings contained under this root convey the sense of expiration, death, and even killing. This is undoubtedly related to the idea that all has been decided and decreed, which is often connected with the role and presence of Allah. Perhaps the semantic development that has taken place is one from "sense of expiration" to "passing, finality." Note the common expression *quḍiʾa al-ʾamr* ("the thing is decided, decreed"). See *Tahḏīb* 9. 211; *Ṣiḥāḥ* 2. 316–17; *Lisān* 20. 47–49; *Tāj* 10. 296–97; *Maqāyīs* 5. 99–100.

[97] Lane, 2989; Hava, 612. Driver's dependence upon this third verbal form is itself problematic since the third conjugation is always secondary and must be late. Related to this is his decision to propose an Arabic cognate which has a weak third radical for a hollow Hebrew root. The Hebrew word should first be compared to Arabic *qāḍa* ("to destroy").

[98] It appears that perhaps Driver has taken his meaning from Dozy (2. 362), who translates the third form of the verb as "to conclude a treaty or agreement with someone" (*conclure un traité avec quelqu'un*). An important point to keep in mind when using Dozy, however, is that much of his data is based upon the Arabic of Spain in the Middle Ages. This is not to say that his dictionary is worthless, but it must be used with caution and careful judgment in order to determine whether or not lexical material which is genuinely ancient has been preserved. This point will be explored more fully in the next chapter. Dozy's entry under this verbal form is a case in point. The literary reference it quotes for support is of Spanish origin and of such an inconclusive nature as to throw the meaning of the word into serious doubt. It contains a nominal, not verbal, form of the root that may more properly refer to judgment rather than to agreement. This is seen in the fact that there is a judge present in the scene described who plays a key role in the proceedings. As noted above, this severely weakens Driver's position. It should be pointed out that although the Arabic evidence suggests that his proposal should be discarded, it appears as an alternative reading in the *NEB*. The later revision of the *NEB*, the *REB*, does away with this alternative reading.

2.3.10. MSS I, *massa, yamassu* // *ʾamseh*

In an attempt to render more reasonable the hyperbolic *ʾamseh* of Ps 6:7 ("with my tears I cause my bed to dissolve") Guillaume has offered the meaning "wet" based on this Arabic verb.[99] A careful analysis of the sources reveals that the data cannot sustain his contention. All dictionaries are agreed that the primary sense of the root is to touch and feel. This has carried over into the modern usage as well.[100] There is some scanty evidence that links the verb with water, but a careful look at these citations shows that they are still closely identified with touching, the primary sense of the root. These are found in the first and fourth forms of the verb. The first form can mean "(the water) wetted (the body)," and the fourth can translate "one caused (water) to wet (the body)." It is significant that in both cases it is the body and not some inanimate object that is the object of the verb. This highlights the fact that it is the sensation of feeling and touch of the water that is central and not the simple fact of wetting.

The case is clinched when we note that a sense connected with water is found in several nominal forms of the root and in each of these instances it is once again the experience of touching or tasting it that is primary. Among the meanings are "water that is reached by the hands," "water taken by extended hands," "water that removes thirst," and "water that is bitter, salty and undrinkable."[101]

Our study has uncovered two key facts related to the root *massa*. First of all, the meaning "to wet" plays a very minor, perhaps inconsequential, role within the context of its entire semantic range. Secondly, even in those nominal forms where "water" is a primary signification it is its feel and taste that is highlighted.[102]

The above examples have been cited as evidence for the existence of tunnel vision among biblical scholars who make use of Arabic data in their work.

[99] Guillaume, 2. 22.

[100] *Jamhara* 1. 95; *Ṣiḥāḥ* 2. 495–96; *Maqāyīs* 5. 271; Lane, 2711; Wehr, 906.

[101] Several texts clearly point up the connection between water and taste. A verse of poetry in al-Azharī reads "If you were water you would be neither fresh tasting nor *masūs* (bitter/salty)." (*Tahḏīb* 12. 324) See also the *Qāmūs* (2. 261) which describes one of the nominal forms as "a flavor of water."

[102] The meaning of touch and feeling also appears to be extended metaphorically in the root. The word *mamsūs* (*Tāj* 4. 247), literally "touched," refers to a type of mental illness in a way that corresponds perfectly to English usage. This is probably a development from the well known word for madness that refers to "being touched by the *jinn*" (*majnūn*). L. L. Grabbe makes this same point in *Comparative Philology and the Text of Job: A Study in Methodology* (Missoula, MT: Scholars Press, 1977) 50.

While this phenomenon does not characterize the work of all scholars engaged in such study, or of all work of the scholars cited, it has appeared frequently enough that the general observations made at the beginning of this chapter seem justified. The three forms of tunnel vision mentioned there – isolation of a rare or secondary meaning, dependence upon one source for a meaning, and disregard for the semantic field of a given word or root – have all been documented. The rich treasure of Arabic lexicography is not well used in such a fashion.

CHAPTER 3

Restricting the Semantic History: Myopia

The previous chapter attempted to identify some of the ways in which biblical scholars, in making use of the vast resources of the Arabic language, have focused too narrowly on particular forms or meanings and have consequently misread or wrongly interpreted their data. In their work they have been guilty of a type of tunnel vision which fails to take into account the surrounding context and does not examine the material with a wide-angle lens. This chapter will try to explore a related phenomenon which may also be described in terminology borrowed from the language of sight. Whereas the previous chapter was concerned with problems in peripheral vision the present one will be interested in difficulties related to depth perception. It will attempt to prove the existence of a scholarly myopia on the part of some who have made use of Arabic sources in their work in biblical Hebrew lexicography.

The most common symptom of this myopic condition is an analysis of the Arabic data that stops at a particular point in time along the continuum of the development of the language and does not extend back to the earliest sources available. There are varying degrees of this scholarly nearsightedness: some treat only modern forms and meanings of words, while others go back as far as the late medieval period but no further. Regardless of their relative depth of vision, however, they all share in the inability to lengthen their range of sight to include the earliest Arabic sources.

The results of such a methodological flaw can be disastrous. In effect, we have a situation similar to the one encountered in the previous chapter as, once again, the context of a word is passed over. This time, however, it is the historical or diachronic context that is ignored. This leads to an inability to see how a particular form functions historically in the lexicographic or semantic development of the root. Consequently, such important factors as the point in time at which a form enters the language, dialectal shifts and variants, changes in meaning over time, and usage that is restricted to a particular time or locale are missed and do not enter into the discussion in determining the relative value of a particular form or meaning for biblical Hebrew.

All of the examples that will be studied in this chapter do not go back far enough in the Arabic sources. They make no mention at all of the earliest dictionaries but rely, for the most part, on modern sources. Some of these sources are more dependable than others but all of them suffer from a common shortcoming: while they are not always inaccurate, they are always incomplete. A comparison between them and the Arabic dictionaries of the earliest period highlights this fact. While some of the more recent dictionaries may contain older meanings, such meanings are typically given out of context without any of the details found in the earlier sources. They are also mixed in with modern meanings, often with no indication of their chronological relationship. This is a particularly critical point for the type of work these lexicographers are undertaking. Since all of these studies are concerned with interpreting words found in biblical Hebrew, the age of an Arabic form or meaning is a key question. If no evidence exists that can trace an Arabic meaning to the earliest stages of the language, its relevance for biblical Hebrew is virtually nonexistent. This points out the crippling effect scholarly myopia can have: dependence on modern dictionaries makes determination of the age of a particular form or meaning an impossible task.

In some cases, the reason for these scholars' exclusive use of more contemporary sources is glaringly apparent. Their knowledge of Arabic is of such a limited nature that consultation of the earliest dictionaries, which are written entirely in Arabic, is not an option for them. Consequently, they must rely on works like Dozy, Hava, Wehr, and a host of other dictionaries that give the meanings of Arabic forms in European languages and are therefore more accessible. The risk involved in this approach, namely the fact that these dictionaries usually give incomplete information that is out of context and often more concerned with modern or geographically limited usage, has already been mentioned. An exception to this situation is Lane's *Arabic English Lexicon* which, in its first six volumes at least, offers a comprehensive treatment of the Arabic data and is a reliable resource. Surprisingly, however, few, if any, of the examples of scholarly myopia that we will now consider appear to have made use of Lane's work.

The examples treated in this chapter will be listed under one of two categories, depending on the type of myopia that is most prevalent in each:

1) Reliance Upon Temporally Limited Evidence

Some proposals are based on Arabic forms or meanings that are present only at later stages in the development of the language. Included here are examples which rely upon Arabic evidence which first appears in the late medieval or modern periods but is not found in the earliest lexicographical sources. This obviously renders their applicability to biblical Hebrew highly questionable.

2) Reliance Upon Geographically Limited Evidence

A related phenomenon is the construction of an argument that is based on forms or meanings that are found in only a small part of the Arabic speaking world. These are usually examples of highly idiosyncratic usage that is unique to a particular region and not found anywhere else. Once again, the relevance of such data for biblical Hebrew lexicography is severely limited.

It should be observed that many of the examples we will now examine can fit into either of these two categories since they are both recent additions to the Arabic lexicon and limited to specific places. This is to be expected. It is the nature of a language like Arabic, which covers a wide geographic area and is used by people in a vast range of social and cultural contexts, that additions to the lexical and semantic depository in the course of its evolution will not always be universal. Both temporal and geographic limitation will therefore often exist side by side. Consequently, the categorization that follows should not be taken to suggest that these are two unique types of problems that have little in common other than a tendency toward what has been termed here "myopia." The division between the two is noted only to highlight more clearly two important aspects of the same problem that is often encountered in the use of Arabic in biblical Hebrew lexicography.

1) Reliance Upon Temporally Limited Evidence

3.1.1. Tʿ I, *taʿataʿa // nittāʿû*

The origin of the word *nittāʿû,* a verbal form which refers to the teeth of young lions in Job 4:10, is somewhat unclear and the word is usually translated "broken" either on the basis of a possible Aramaic form or an emendation to *nittāṣû*. Guillaume suggests the translation "the teeth of the young lions are knocked out" and sees the above Arabic verb as the key to interpretation.[1] There are a number of problems with this proposal. First of all, the equivalence is not a smooth one from the lexicographical point of view.[2] The context indicates a passive meaning and the vocalization of the Hebrew verb points in the direction of a *Niphal* form of a primae *nun* root. In order to adopt Guillaume's suggestion, then, one must explain the troubling absence of the initial *nun* in the Arabic form.

Equally problematic is the meaning Guillaume assigns to this Arabic verb. He acknowledges that the sense "to pull teeth" is a specifically modern Egyptian meaning and it is thus designated in Hava's dictionary.[3] Guillaume is correct in stating that violent action is an important sense for this Arabic root, but only the dialect forms seem to connect this violence with pulling teeth. None of the older dictionaries make any mention of this at all in their treatments of the root.[4] Rather, they speak generally of any action or activity that is of a violent nature.

The meaning "to pull out a tooth" appears, then, to be a later development found in the Egyptian dialect.[5] Although the exact details of its semantic formation are unclear, there could be some connection with yet another sense of the verb that is well attested in the earliest dictionaries, namely, with reference to an animal falling down or being stuck and sinking in the sand.

Regardless of the origin of this particular meaning of the Arabic dialect verb, the key point to note is that it is a late addition to the semantic range of the root. As such it is of little, if any, value to a discussion on a form that is found in biblical Hebrew. Guillaume has isolated this one recent meaning out of its context and applied it in this case because it seems to offer a clever solution to a problem of biblical Hebrew lexicography.

[1] Guillaume, *Hebrew and Arabic Lexicography III*, 5. Originally published in *Abr Nahrain* 3 (1962–63).

[2] On the most basic level, it should be observed that the juxtaposition of these two roots is *a priori* improbable since reduplicated quadriliteral roots mostly have a life of their own and hardly ever interact with triliteral ones.

[3] Hava, 59. According to Hava the Egyptian verb can also mean "to pull out a stone."

[4] *Ṣiḥāḥ* 1. 142; *Jamhara* 1. 130; *Qāmūs* 3. 10; *Lisān* 9. 383–84; *Tāj* 5. 291; *Maqāyīs* 1. 338. Another important sense under this root is that of stuttering or repeating words in an uncontrollable way.

[5] This meaning is also found in other modern dialects. *HALAT* 694 lists this Arabic verb and meaning as a cognate but only cites A. Barthélemy's *Dictionnaire Arabe-Français* as its source for this. This dictionary, first compiled in 1935, treats only usage found in the dialects of Syria, Palestine and Lebanon.

3.1.2. TLL I, *talla, yatallu* // *tôlālênû*

G. R. Driver proposes a revocalization of the word *tôlālênû* to *tôlĕlênû* in Ps 137:3 and suggests that the Arabic verb *talla* will support his translation "those who took us prisoners."[6] Had he gone to the earliest Arabic dictionaries to examine their treatment of the root he would have discovered that they do not contain this meaning. It rather appears that he has had to base his proposal on more recent sources and even then has not interpreted their data accurately.

The most common meanings that the older sources have for *talla* are all related to the theme of throwing someone or something upon the ground. A related sense that is frequent is that of lying on one's side or stomach on the ground. There is not a single mention of prison or being taken prisoner. When the referent is an individual it is the physical position of the person upon the ground, and not his or her status as prisoner or anything else, that is clearly the focus of the word. This is seen in the *Tahḏīb*'s definition of a nominal form as "laziness," which obviously stems from the lazy one's perennial horizontal position.[7]

Driver cites Dozy as the source for the definition he puts forth, but there is a major difficulty with his use of Dozy. The expressions that he quotes from Dozy unmistakably indicate that the "prisoner" part of the definition is not a part of this verb's meaning. In each case there is a definite object or prepositional phrase which designate the prison as the place one is cast "thrown down," or, as Dozy's word *traîner* suggests, "dragged to."[8] In other words, according to the Arabic sources, the verbal form alone is not sufficient to warrant a translation that refers to someone being taken prisoner. This must be explicitly stated with a specific reference to a prison or some related word.

Through his reliance upon Dozy to support his suggestion, Driver has given a distorted sense of the meaning of this Arabic verb. The grammatical structure of the expressions he cites should offer sufficient warning to Driver that his interpretation is unsound, but his more serious error lies in not taking into account the data regarding this form found in the earlier Arabic dictionaries.

[6] G. R. Driver, "Notes on the Psalms," *JTS* 36 (1935) 155.

[7] *Tahḏīb* 14. 251; see also *Jamhara* 1. 42; *Tāj* 7. 240–42; Lane, 310–11. The *Maqāyīs* (1. 339) describes well the phenomenon of contradictory meanings coexisting in the same root with its observation that *talla* can mean both "raising up" and its opposite (*al-intiṣābu wa ḍidduhu*).

[8] The three expressions Driver quotes are *ʾamara bitillihi illā maḥbasihi* ("he ordered him to be cast into his prison"), *tulla illā maṣraʿihi* ("he was led off to his place of execution"), and *tallahu lilḥabs* ("he cast him into prison"). The first two are taken word for word from Dozy but I have not identified the source of the third expression.

His vision has stopped at Dozy and not traced the development and significance of the root as it is found in the older sources.[9]

3.1.3. Jʿ R I, *jaʿara, yajʿaru* // *gāʿar*

In an article which treats the Hebrew root *gāʿar* A. A. MacIntosh tries to gather cognate evidence to support his view that the root denotes growling and roaring.[10] His use of the Arabic data, however, focuses on more modern meanings of the verb and ignores some important aspects of the root.

He rightly notes that the most common meaning of the Arabic verb *jaʿara* has to do with passing excrement.[11] He quickly concludes, however, that this sense does not illuminate the meaning of the Hebrew root. More important for his purposes are two meanings he cites from modern usage. He identifies *jaʿara* as meaning "to bellow" in Syrian Arabic and "to snarl" in colloquial Egyptian. Although he does not explicitly draw out their connection to the Hebrew root, he gives the impression that this Arabic evidence helps to support his conclusion. This is a serious mistake, given the late nature of the meanings. He cites Hava's dictionary as his source for the Syrian data and mentions a private communication with someone who told him of the Egyptian usage. The latter source is particularly problematic. Private information treating colloquial Arabic is not a very reliable basis for the type of argument MacIntosh tries to construct. Beyond this difficulty is the fact that, as we have noted, none of the authoritative Arabic sources speak of growling or roaring being part of the root.[12]

Hava alerts us to the reason for the inclusion of the meaning "to bellow" under this root, but MacIntosh ignores this reference in his discussion. Hava

[9] We see a similar misreading of the sources for this root in Guillaume's treatment of it in *Hebrew and Arabic Lexicography IV* (10) where it is given the meaning "to lift up, cast up." Guillaume acknowledges that this is an Egyptian meaning and it is so designated in Hava (61). This creates an unusual situation in which evidence from modern Arabic is used to give a word the exact opposite meaning it has in the early Arabic sources. To propose, as Guillaume does, that this can have any bearing on the meaning of a cognate biblical Hebrew form is inaccurate.

[10] A. A. MacIntosh, "A Consideration of Hebrew גער," *VT* 19 (1969) 472–73.

[11] According to the dictionaries the verb is used to refer to the passing of dung by an animal that has claws or talons. See, for example, *Ṣiḥāḥ* 1. 194; *Tahḏīb* 1. 362–63; *Qāmūs* 1. 405–06; *Tāj* 3. 102–03; *Maqāyīs* 1. 463. There is no reference to growling or roaring.

[12] It is particularly interesting that while one of the nominal forms carries the meaning "hyena" this does not appear to be due to the noises the animal makes. Rather, the sources are specific in stating that the animal is called a *jaʿār* because of the abundance of its dung. If roaring or other animal noises were a part of this root's semantic range one would expect to see some indication of it here in reference to the hyena, which is well known for its vocal capabilities.

observes that the meaning "to bellow" is actually from the root *jaʾara*, which has a *hamza* rather than an *ʿayn* as the middle root radical.[13] On this point Hava is surely correct, since some of the most basic meanings under the root *jaʾara* have to do with animals lowing or people calling out.[14] This observation totally negates MacIntosh's theory, since it is clear that what he has cited is not a proper reading of the reliable data on the root *jaʿara* but a colloquial Syrian variation that substitutes that root for another (*jaʾara*) while preserving its original meaning. He cites Hava's dictionary in a footnote so he must be aware of the fact that it places the meaning "to bellow" with the root *jaʾara* and not the root he is studying. But he never addresses this issue in the article. Because this Arabic evidence, however suspicious, suits his needs and confirms his theory he uses it as further support.[15]

3.1.4. SLK I, *salaka, yasluku* // *ʾašlîk*

In a very obvious example of scholarly myopia with regard to the Arabic sources G. R. Driver uses this verb with the definition "to save, rescue" to defend his translation of the Hebrew word *ʾašlîk* in Job 29:17.[16] This then gives the passage the meaning "I rescued the prey from his teeth." As the following analysis will demonstrate, this proposal is based on extremely late evidence, and an examination of the more authoritative sources suggests that the Arabic data actually support a meaning opposite the one Driver has proposed.

Driver identifies the sense of drawing a sword from a scabbard as an important one which highlights the central role of removal and deliverance in the root. However, the notion of removal, salvation or deliverance (from either a situation or an object) is not found in any of the Arabic dictionaries. In fact, the opposite sense of entry or insertion is consistently found. This is seen in such basic and well attested meanings as "to enter a place," "to go along a road," and "to insert something into something else."[17] The sources are unanimous in seeing entry rather than removal as the primary meaning of the root. Beyond this, there are some important citations in the dictionaries that are in direct opposition to Driver's sense of salvation and deliverance. For instance, the

[13] Hava, 91. Wahrmund 1. 439 makes the same observation.

[14] Lane, 369–70. This is also seen in Wehr, 110, 127.

[15] It is therefore unfortunate that *HALAT* 192 lists the Arabic verb *jaʿara* as a cognate form and gives it the meaning "to moo, low." The source of these data is not given.

[16] G. R. Driver, "Problems in Job," *AJSL* 52 (1935–36), 163.

[17] Lane, 1411–12.

Ṣiḥāḥ quotes a passage from the *Qur'n* (26:200) in which Allah says "thus we have caused it (disbelief) to enter (*salaknāhu*) into the hearts of the unbelievers." Elsewhere, the *Tahḏīb* quotes al-Laith as saying "Allah leads (*yusliku* – a causative form) the unbelievers into Gehenna; that is, he makes them enter into it."[18] In both these citations the verb refers to the entry of something (or someone) for the purpose of destruction, not the removal of something for salvation.

Driver's translation is based entirely upon data found in Dozy's dictionary, and a careful study of it reveals its very late origin and relative uselessness for a study such as Driver's. Dozy lists "to escape" (*se sauver*) and "to save" (*sauver*) as meanings for the first and second forms of the verb, respectively, but his sources are all late and/or colloquial.[19] The Arabic verb *salaka* has the general meaning of passing or proceeding. Other meanings are interpretations aided by the use of appropriate prepositions.[20]

3.1.5. FŠK̲ I, *fašak̲a, yafšak̲u // pāśaʿ*

The Hebrew root *pāśaʿ* is only found a few times in the MT (Isa 27:4; 1 Sam 20:3; 1 Chr 19:4) and in each place it is connected with the sense of stepping or marching. Guillaume sees a cognate Arabic form in this verb to which he assigns the same sense.[21] The problems with his proposal are ones with which we are now well familiar. In the first place, there is a difficulty regarding the third radical letter of the two roots since he equates Hebrew *ʿayin* with Arabic *k̲*. This runs against the normal equivalences followed in discussions of the relationship between Arabic and Hebrew, and among Semitic languages in general, and raises a serious initial question about the validity of his proposal.[22]

[18] *Ṣiḥāḥ* 1. 605; *Tahḏīb* 10. 62; see also *Lisān* 12. 327; *Jamhara* 3. 45; *Maqāyīs* 3. 97.

[19] Dozy 1. 676–77. In a telling omission, Driver has failed to mention the fact that Dozy also includes the much better attested meaning "to enter" under the first verbal form.

[20] This is another example of a suggestion by Driver that we have determined to be very questionable being accepted into the text of the *NEB*. The text of Job 29:17b reads "and I rescued the prey from his teeth." *REB*, the revision of *NEB*, changes this to read "and (I) wrested the prey from his teeth."

[21] Guillaume, *Hebrew and Arabic Lexicography*, 4. 12.

[22] This type of unorthodox pairing of Hebrew and Arabic sounds/graphemes is something that is characteristic of Guillaume's work. He bases this practice on a work entitled *Kitāb al-Ibdāl* by the tenth century scholar al-Ḥalabī, which treats the phenomenon of the interchange of consonants in Arabic. This is a well documented aspect of the Arabic language, but Guillaume appeals to it much too frequently as support for his proposals. In the present case, for instance,

Of more interest for our purposes, and more damaging to his suggestion, is the fact that the meaning Guillaume assigns to this verb is a late development within the root and therefore has nothing to add to a study of the biblical Hebrew form. A number of the earliest dictionaries, including the *Ṣiḥāḥ*, *Jamhara*, and *Qāmūs*, do not even have an entry for this root. Those which do are unanimous in making no reference whatsoever to any meaning having to do with walking or marching. They have it refer either to slapping/hitting someone on the head or to a game children play that has the goal of deceiving or tricking one's opponent.[23]

As he has done with other examples we have studied, Guillaume clearly indicates that the meaning he cites for this Arabic verb is of Syrian origin.[24] Its absence in the early sources leads us to conclude that it is modern, and an examination of some of the dictionaries treating more recent usage confirms this. In several places in his work Guillaume refers to Hava as an extremely important and valuable resource and, although he does not acknowledge it in this case, Hava appears to be his source for this verbal form also.[25] In the same way, both Wehr and Dozy contain meanings for the verb that are related to the theme of walking and striding and these are clearly modern innovations.[26]

3.1.6. QLW/Y V, *taqallā, yataqallā // niqleh*

To support the translation "fever" for the word *niqleh* in Ps 38:8 ("my loins burn with fever"), G. R. Driver cites the Arabic expression *taqallā ʿala firāšihi* which he translates "to be feverish, restless in bed."[27] With this citation and translation he has fallen victim to myopia, but a type different from that typically encountered.

The expression Driver cites is found in Hava, which he gives as his source,

---

he assumes an interchange between the Arabic *k̲* and Hebrew *ʿayin* and therefore argues that this Hebrew root and Arabic *fašak̲a* are, in effect, the same root. The illegitimacy of this approach need not detain us since we shall see there are more clear-cut reasons why his proposal regarding this Arabic form should be discarded.

[23] See, for example, *Lisān* 4. 14, *Tāj* 2. 273 and *Maqāyīs* 4. 504 which treat the verbal form, and *Tahd̲īb* 7. 89 which mentions only a nominal form.

[24] Wahrmund (2. 412) also indicates that the meaning "einen Schritt machen" is recent.

[25] Hava, 563.

[26] Wehr, 714; Dozy 2. 268. This error has been perpetuated by *HALAT* (920), which, although it does not directly cite Guillaume, refers to Hava's meanings having to do with long strides and spreading the legs. It also mentions a similar proposal put forth by G. R. Driver in *Bib* 32 (1951) 193–94.

[27] G. R. Driver, "Notes on the Psalms," 150.

and it is also present in the earliest Arabic dictionaries. But Driver depends solely on the data in Hava's work to translate the phrase and this leads to a distorted reading. As the following analysis will try to show, it appears that Driver's shortsightedness in this case is due to his reliance upon one modern dictionary for information on the word. Had he gone back to examine the earlier Arabic sources which treat it in more detail he would have recognized the error of his proposal.

From the outset it should be noted that Driver is interpreting, and not simply quoting, the data found in Hava. This is seen in the fact that the word "fever" never appears in Hava in connection with this or any other form of the root. The only translation that is given for the expression is "to be restless in bed."[28] It appears that Driver has drawn what seems to be a logical connection between being restless in bed and being feverish, based on meanings found for other words under the root. One of the most common meanings for the first verbal form is "to fry in a pan," and there are several nominal forms that refer to the frying pan, skillet and places where frying is done.[29] Seeing this as the primary semantic field of the root Driver has probably linked the sense of frying with fever and interpreted this as the cause of nocturnal restlessness.

This reading of the data is plausible and seemingly coherent within the narrow confines of Hava's entry on the root. But once we extend our vision and study other sources, the logic of Driver's interpretation is shown to be flawed. The older dictionaries, along with Hava, note that the sense of frying is an important one for the root and they also indicate that the fifth form of the verb can mean "to hate."[30] They also contain the expression *taqallā ʿala firāšihi*, which is central to Driver's proposal, but they treat it in a way that Hava does not. They clearly state the reason for the person's restlessness in bed and, in a blow to Driver's theory, assert it has nothing to do with fever. In fact, just as we saw with Hava, the word "fever" never appears in any of the older Arabic dictionaries' treatments of this root. According to these sources, a person *taqallā* on the bed when he or she is preoccupied with an important matter and spends the whole night awake, tossing and turning as if on a frying

[28] Hava, 626.

[29] The form being studied here, *taqallā*, is the fifth verbal form of the root. It is unclear why Driver appeals to the fifth form, which is derivative, when the first form contains meanings which support his proposal. "To fry" is close enough to heat and fever to make his reliance on the metaphorical senses of form five unnecessary.

[30] *Ṣiḥāḥ* 2. 339; *Lisān* 20. 60–61. Hava also has the meaning "to hate" for the fifth form but Driver does not mention this.

pan.[31] The cause of the restlessness, then, is not fever but worry and anxiety. Driver is right to see a connection between the expression and the references to frying but he has misinterpreted the connection: it is not the heat of the pan that is the point of comparison but rather the action of being tossed and turned on the skillet.

This is an excellent example of the type of myopia which can result from exclusively using modern dictionaries in one's study of Arabic data. It is not that Hava's dictionary cannot be trusted in this case; it is just incomplete. It contains all the meanings the older sources have but it gives them out of context. One's vision must be deepened to include earlier works which usually go into more detail and determine more precisely the meaning and function of a word within the Arabic language. Driver's mistake this time is not an inappropriate use of a modern form or meaning but reliance on a modern usage dictionary which leads to a distorted interpretation of a well attested form and meaning.

3.1.7. KWY, *al-kuy // kî*

J. Reider believes the second half of Job 39:27 is weak from the point of view of parallelism and suggests there might be a word "hidden" behind the Hebrew particle *kî* which is related to the word *nāšer* ("eagle") in the first part of the verse.[32] He identifies the Arabic word cited above as the missing link which completes the parallelism and gives the Hebrew word the meaning "pelican." The only flaw in his theory is that this link is also missing in the Arabic sources.

None of the major dictionaries consulted contain this form or meaning. The only place it is found is Dozy, which Reider has cited. It should be apparent by now that dependence solely upon Dozy for evidence related to biblical Hebrew is precarious at best and his sources must be carefully studied to determine their usefulness and worth. Reider has apparently chosen either not to do this or to ignore the results of his findings. As usual, Dozy relies upon works of the late medieval period and later for his data under this entry. One is a history of the Mamluk sultans (1254-1517), the second is the glossary which De Jong added to Thaᶜālibī's collection *Laṭā'if al-Maᶜārif* in 1867 and the third is

[31] This is explained very clearly in *Tahḏīb* 9. 296. The same idea is found in the *Lisān* (20. 62), which says the fifth form of the verb refers to someone being fidgety or nervous (*yatamalmal*) in bed.

[32] J. Reider, "Etymological Studies in Biblical Hebrew," *VT* 4 (1954) 294.

the work of Ibn al-Baiṭār, which Dozy says is distinguished by its extremely poor quality of scholarship and the fact that it is full of Spanish and Greek words.[33] This is very shaky ground that Reider has chosen as the basis for his proposal.[34]

3.1.8. LHṬ I, *lahaṭa, yalhaṭu // lōhăṭîm*

G. R. Driver proposes an unconvincing reading of a word in Ps 57:5 by referring to this Arabic verb to support the meaning "to gobble up" for *lōhăṭîm*.[35] Once again, a careful reading of his proposal and analysis of the sources he quotes for support leads to the conclusion that he has drawn principally on modern dialectal Arabic to support his contention.

The first point that needs to be made is that the root *lahaṭa* does not appear in some of the most important Arabic dictionaries including *Jamhara*, *Qāmūs*, and *Tāj*. The most common meaning in those sources where it is found has to do with slapping or hitting someone.[36] We find no references to Driver's meaning "to gobble up" anywhere in the early sources. It is only Dozy's dictionary, which Driver cites for support, that lists this meaning. In fact, it is the only meaning offered for the root.[37] Yet, again, the sources Dozy gives are of more recent vintage and are of little worth in a discussion considering the meaning of a biblical Hebrew word. He cites three sources for this meaning. The first is Bocthor's *Dictionnaire Française-Arabe* from the mid-ninteenth century. In his preface Dozy states that this is a dictionary of the modern language and is often helpful in understanding usage of the late Middle Ages.[38] The second is the *Muḥīṭ al-Muḥīṭ* of al-Bustānī, and Dozy also comments on this work and says it should be used with care and prudence since al-Bustānī has included a large number of non-classical words and meanings as well as terms from the Syrian dialect.[39] The third, which defines the verb as "to swallow" (*avaler*), is from an article published in Copenhagen in 1872 which Dozy

[33] Dozy 2. 503. See also Dozy's critical remarks on Ibn al-Baitār's work (1. xviii).

[34] Reider's selective use of Dozy's dictionary is also seen in his reference to P. Smith's *Thesaurus Syriacus* which he says supports the reading "pelican." Dozy notes this but believes that this might be due to confusion with a similar Arabic word which changes one letter. Reider makes no mention of this at all and therefore gives the impression that the evidence is clear and unambiguous. The only meaning the *Maqāyīs* (5. 145) has for this Arabic root is "to burn."

[35] G. R. Driver, "Studies in the Vocabulary of the Old Testament IV," *JTS* 33 (1932). 39.

[36] *Ṣiḥāḥ* 2. 645; *Lisān* 9. 270–71; *Maqāyīs* 5. 216.

[37] Dozy 1. 552.

[38] Dozy 1. xi.

[39] Dozy 1. xi. Haywood (109) makes a similar point regarding this source.

describes as a listing of popular words (*mots vulgaires*) which the author has found. In short, Driver has based his proposal on extremely shaky grounds by appealing to very late evidence that is not attested at all in the older sources.[40]

Further support for this being a more modern meaning comes from Hava's dictionary which does list the meaning "to gobble," but has the siglum indicating the Syrian dialect next to it.[41] Hava also adds a comment which helps to solve the mystery of how this meaning came to be identified with the root. He suggests that the initial letter has been changed and the meaning "to gobble" in fact comes from the root *rahaṭa*. An examination of the early dictionaries suggests that this is indeed the case. Some of the most important witnesses give the meaning of *rahaṭa* as "to eat much or quickly."[42] What has probably happened is that certain dialects changed the initial letter of the root, thereby altering its form in a way that invites identification with the root *lahaṭa* while preserving its original meaning. The sources cited in Dozy reflect this situation and this, of course, renders them less than helpful as guides in helping to determine the meaning of the Hebrew word which Driver studies.

3.1.9. HLK V, *tahallaka, yatahallaku // hithallākĕtā*

The word *hithallākĕtā* of Ezek 28:14 is usually translated "walk" but G. R. Driver prefers the sense "to swagger, strut proudly" and enlists this Arabic verb, the fifth form of the verb *halaka*, for support.[43] He does not cite his source for this meaning and a study of the primary dictionaries indicates that it cannot have come from any of them. Some of them, including *Jamhara* and *Ṣiḥāḥ*, do not make any reference to the fifth form at all. Those dictionaries that do mention the fifth form appear to all originate from the same ancient source: a saying by a certain ʿArrām who says "I was *atahallaku* in the desert." It is clear that the meaning of the word in these dictionaries is quite different

[40] This situation is also reflected in the treatment of the Hebrew word found in *HALAT* (495). It also proposes this Arabic verb as a cognate and gives it the meaning "to eat quickly." Its source for this meaning is listed as Barthélemy's Arabic-French dictionary, which reflects only dialectal usage from Syria, Palestine and Lebanon. Wahrmund (2.657) also marks the meaning "gierig verschlingen" as a neologism.

[41] Hava, 698. Along with this meaning Hava has the more original and early attested one of "to slap, hit" that was mentioned above.

[42] See, for example, *Qāmūs* 2.375 which defines the verbal form as "to eat quickly"; also *Lisān* 9.186–88 and *Tāj* 5.145, which defines it as "to eat much or quickly." This is also supported in modern literary Arabic as seen in Wehr who translates *lahaṭa* as "to slap" (881) and *rahaṭa* as "to gobble, gulp greedily" (362).

[43] G. R. Driver, "Ezechiel: Linguistic and Textual Problems," 159.

from that put forth by Driver. In fact, they offer a meaning that gives the opposite sense of Driver's. The *Tahḏīb* goes on to explain the word by stating (it is unclear if these are the words of al-Azhārī, the compiler of the dictionary, or they are from ʿArrām) "that is, I was going about in it (the desert) like one confused and hesitant."[44] The pride and swagger which Driver identifies in the form are not found and have been identified in the earliest Arabic sources as uncertainty and trepidation. In effect, if one were to argue for a meaning of the Hebrew word based on the primary Arabic evidence one would have to propose a meaning which suggests confusion, not confidence. But this would go against the context of the passage in which God is speaking of the king of Tyre as a model of perfection.

If such is the situation regarding this verbal form, on what is Driver's suggestion based? Although he does not acknowledge his source, it is clear that he has taken this meaning from Hava's dictionary, where the very Arabic expression Driver cites ("he swaggered in his gait") is found.[45] Hava gives no indication that this meaning is a dialectal variant, but given the nature of his dictionary and the fact that this meaning is not supported by any of the earlier sources, one should be somewhat suspicious of it and hesitant to use it in connection with a study treating biblical Hebrew. In all probability this is a further example of lexical myopia which isolates a more recent meaning of an Arabic word.

2) Reliance Upon Geographically Limited Evidence

3.2.1. BṬN, *al-baṭn* // *ʾŏnîyâ*

In an article in which he analyzes the book of Jonah, F. Zimmerman suggests seeing the boat Jonah travels in as a womb symbol.[46] To support this notion he appeals to evidence from Latin and Greek which, he says, shows that in ancient times people naturally saw a connection between "womb" and "ship." He acknowledges that Hebrew usage does not reflect this identification of these

[44] *Tahḏīb* 6, 16; see also *Lisān* 12, 399 and *Tāj* 7, 196, which quote the same saying and offer the same meaning. This sense fits with the well attested primary meaning of the root connected with perishing and destruction (*Maqāyīs* 6, 62–63).

[45] Hava, 833. A further blow to Driver's proposal is the fact that Hava claims the sixth verbal form of the root (*tahālaka*) can also be used with the same meaning. The expression he gives and Driver cites is *tahallaka* (or *tahālaka*) *fī mašīhi*.

[46] F. Zimmerman, "Problems and Solutions in the Book of Jonah," *Judaism* 40 (1991), 582–83.

two ideas, but in an effort to locate it in another Semitic language he states that "in Arabic, however, *batn* (*sic*), "womb," undoubtedly has an association with *mubtanah* (*sic*), "sailing vessel" (in the dialect of Syria)."

His treatment of the Arabic data is riddled with problems. In terms of orthography, his transliteration of the Arabic terms is extremely sloppy. The correct letters of this Arabic root are *bṭn* and not, as he indicates, *btn*. Similarly, the second word he cites is properly spelled *mubaṭṭanah*, not *mubtanah*. Of more importance for our purposes is the question of the meanings he assigns to these words. He gives Hava as his source for these translations but there is a significant problem encountered with each. Regarding the first word, the meaning "womb" is never found in Hava's dictionary, and, as he notes, the second word is unique to the Syrian dialect.[47] This raises some fundamental questions about the validity of Zimmerman's proposal that can only be answered by turning to the older Arabic sources to examine how they treat this root.

Although it is not the only meaning the word can have, there is older evidence to support the translation "womb" for *baṭn*. The *Tahḏīb*, for instance, says "a woman delivers what is in her *baṭn* when she gives birth" and "a hen delivers what is in her *baṭn* when she lays eggs."[48] More problematic is the second word (*mubaṭṭanah*), which is clearly a modern form as seen in the fact that none of the older dictionaries list it in their entries under the root.[49] Its absence in the earliest Arabic sources undermines Zimmerman's theory and negates the connection he claims exists between the two meanings in the Arabic language. Most probably *mubaṭṭanah* is a purely descriptive term, like the English "pot-bellied," which refers to the curvature of the sides of the vessel and then takes the place of the noun. It is therefore not a word which describes the vessel itself but its shape.

In effect, Zimmerman has set up a false equation. Although there may be indications that "womb" and "ship" were associated in Latin and Greek, this does not appear to be the case in Arabic. We see this clearly if we approach the issue from a different direction than Zimmerman. As noted above, the sense "womb" is not the primary meaning of the word *baṭn* which more generally means the interior of any person or object.[50] The primary Arabic root which

[47] Hava, 38.

[48] *Tahḏīb* 13. 375. The word usually refers more generally to the interior of a person or thing; see, for example, *Qāmūs* 4. 204; *Tāj* 9. 140–42; Lane, 220–21.

[49] Besides the sources mentioned in the previous footnote see also *Ṣiḥāḥ* 1. 98–99. and *Jamhara*.

[50] *Maqāyīs* 1. 259–60.

yields the word for "womb" is *rḥm*, which is a cognate of the Hebrew *reḥem*. Since this is the root most commonly identified with the sense "womb," if Zimmerman's proposal is correct that Arabic makes a connection between "womb" and "ship" we would expect to find evidence of such a connection here. But there is none to be found since there is not a single reference to anything remotely related to "ship" under the Arabic root *rḥm*.[51]

In his desire to see womb imagery present in the Jonah text Zimmerman has tried to go outside Hebrew to note its presence in another Semitic language. However, his analysis of the Arabic data is flawed. In order to properly establish the Arabic equation "womb = ship" he must find evidence of this in the Arabic root most closely associated with the womb (*rḥm*). Since such evidence does not exist he is forced to find it under another root in which the meaning "womb" has a more secondary status. His more serious mistake is in then basing his entire argument on an Arabic word (*mubaṭṭanah*) that, as a modern Syrian form, is clearly late and unique to a limited geographic area. Had he gone back to the earlier Arabic sources he would have quickly realized that he had been guilty of over-generalization when he wrote "in ancient times people naturally associated in their unconscious mind 'womb' with 'ship'."

3.2.2. JRS II, *jarrasa, yujarrisu // yĕgārĕšû*

The word *yĕgārĕšû* of Zeph 2:4, referring to the fate of Ashdod, is usually given its typical sense of "to drive out," but G. R. Driver believes a more accurate translation would be based on the above Arabic verb, the second form of the root *jrs*, which he translates "to make an example of someone."[52] But certain problems regarding the nature of the Arabic evidence and how Driver attempts to interpret it raise serious doubts about the reliability of his proposal.

Driver claims support for his idea from Lane, whose definition of this form he quotes as "paraded through the street with a bell on his cap, exposed in the pillory." A problem is immediately encountered, however, when we discover that these words never appear in Lane's dictionary. Under the second verbal form Lane has "to render a person notorious or infamous" and then, in parentheses, adds "as, for instance, by parading them and making public proclama-

[51] Lane, 1055–57.

[52] G. R. Driver, "Problems of the Hebrew Text and Language," *Alttestamentliche Studien* (ed. H. Junker & J. Botterweck; Bonn: Peter Hanstein, 1950) 50–51.

tion before them; according to the usage of the verb in the present day."[53] It appears that Lane is giving a modern meaning of the form and this is supported by the fact that he does not give a source for it. Where, then, does the bell on the cap and the pillory come from? All indications suggest that Driver has gotten this sense from Dozy and passed it off as Lane's. Dozy goes into extended detail on this verb and explains how it reflects a practice whereby criminals were paraded through the city with a bell on their hats to bring attention to them and their crimes.[54] He also uses the word "pillory" and others which echo Driver's proposal. Dozy's data suggest that this usage and meaning is decidedly modern since all of his sources are medieval or later. It seems that this practice may have been one that was popular in Spain in the later Middle Ages.[55]

The original meaning of this verb appears to be connected with the sound of a bell and this is probably the sense from which the practice of wearing the cap with the bell is derived. There are also strong indications that the theme of testing or trying a person or object is also a basic part of this root's semantic range.[56] But it does not seem that originally the goal of this test was to embarrass or make a public spectacle of a person. Rather, the emphasis appears to be on improving a person and making him or her a better individual. For example, there is an expression from one ʿAmr which says "time has tested you through experience and made you an expert (*k̲abīr*)."[57] Over time, this idea of testing may have taken on a more negative quality and then eventually united with the other basic meaning referring to the sound of the bell, which combination led to the sense of humiliation and making an example which Driver cites. But it appears that this was a later development that was geographically limited and not part of the original meaning of the root.[58]

[53] Lane, 409.

[54] Dozy 1. 186.

[55] Further evidence for this being a modern meaning is gotten from the dictionaries. Hava (85), for example, has the translation "to bring shame or disgrace upon someone" as modern Syrian usage. See also Wehr (120), who has a number of references to defamation, scandal and disgrace from modern literary Arabic.

[56] *Ṣiḥāḥ* 1. 184; *Qāmūs* 2. 211; *Tahd̲īb* 10. 579; *Maqāyīs* 1. 442.

[57] Cited in *Lisān* 7. 336.

[58] Driver's appeal to Arabic in this instance seems quite unnecessary for another reason. Syriac, which is older than Arabic and more closely related to Hebrew, has the verb *grš*, "to pull," which can also convey the sense "to drive out." This seems to show that the meaning is well attested in NW Semitic.

3.2.3. JRY II, *jarrā, yujarrī* // *yitgārû*

The word *yitgārû* found twice in Dan 11:10 clearly occurs in a military context in which wars and violent takoevers are described. The *NRSV* translation reads: "His sons shall wage war (*yitgārû*) and assemble a multitude of great forces, which shall advance like a flood and pass through, and again shall carry the war (*yitgārû*) as far as his fortress." Kopf cites this Arabic verb as an example of this same sense being expressed in the Arabic root and identifies it as a "confirmation" (*Bestätigung*) of the Hebrew usage.[59] There are some serious problems with this idea. He appears to be basing his conclusion on relatively late data that is geographically restricted and a careful study of the Arabic sources suggests that, actually, there is a more basic sense of this form that is decidedly unmilitaristic.

Dozy is the source Kopf gives for this meaning of the second verbal form and the nominal form *tajriya*, which he translates "incursion, raid of an army into enemy land."[60] Although these meanings are contained in Dozy, they are not very well attested at all. Dozy cites the verbal form from only one source, an Arabic-Latin vocabulary published in Florence in 1871 that is based in turn on a manuscript composed in eastern Spain in the late thirteenth century. Although this is an important source for Dozy's dictionary, he believes there are some difficulties with the text. It should be noted that, given its time and location of composition, we may expect to find many examples of vocabulary and usage that are unique to medieval Spain and this appears to be a case in point. This becomes clearer when we examine Dozy's treatment of the nominal form *tajriya*, which is the only other derivative of the root where a military connotation is found. The sources for this word and its meaning are two: the same Arabic-Latin vocabulary mentioned above and the glossary of Pedro de Alcala of Granada published in 1505. As Dozy himself notes in his discussion of this latter source, we are once again dealing with a text that is characterized by a focus on Arabic forms and meanings that were typical of Spain in the Middle Ages.[61] The fact that Kopf's sense is limited to these two sources in Dozy's dictionary indicates that we are dealing here with usage that is unique to Spain and should not be used as evidence in a discussion on the relevance of the Arabic data for a biblical Hebrew form.

[59] Kopf, "Arabische Etymologien und Parallelen" (1959), 253.

[60] Dozy 1. 190.

[61] For Dozy's description of these two sources and his overview of their strengths and weaknesses see his preface (1. x).

Similarly, the earlier (and later) sources are unanimous in not having any meanings under this root that are in any way related to the type of violent military activity that Kopf has highlighted. The only meaning attested for the second verbal conjugation is "to send an agent or representative" and this is consistently found in all dictionaries.[62] This sense even appears to contradict Kopf's since a main reason a leader might send a messenger or representative to another group would be to avoid military engagement by arriving at a more peaceful settlement. It appears, then, that Kopf is wrong in his suggestion that these Arabic forms can prove useful as a support for his meaning of the Hebrew verb. Although Dozy does contain some information that, at first glance, seems to be relevant, further analysis shows it to be reflective of usage that is unique to a restricted area and a later time. Study of the earlier sources, which make no mention of this meaning and even appear to contradict it, makes this quite clear.

3.2.4. RJᶜ I, *rajaᶜa, yarjiᶜu // rāgaᶜ*

Kopf believes this Arabic verb, to which he gives the meaning "to become," can be a useful cognate form in determining the sense of certain occurrences of the Hebrew verb *rāgaᶜ*. In particular, he bases his translation of the phrase (Job 7:5) *wĕgûš* (Qere) *ᶜāpār ᶜôrî rāgaᶜ wayimmāʾēs* upon it and offers the reading "my skin becomes (like?) earth's crust (*Erdkruste*) which falls apart."[63]

Although one might question Kopf's unusual division of the line, of more immediate concern is the general lack of support for the meaning Kopf assigns to this Arabic verb and then transfers to the Hebrew form. He notes that the primary meaning of the root is "to return" but claims that a semantic development took place which also gave it the sense "to become." But there is no evidence for such a development in the Arabic sources. The earliest dictionaries contain no reference to meanings related to "become" and their entries under the root primarily revolve around the more basic theme of "return".[64] The same thing is true of sources like Hava and Wehr which reflect more recent usage.

[62] See, for example, *Tahḏīb* 11. 172–74 and *Lisān* 18. 154–55; *Maqāyīs*, 1. 448. Note also the reference to the noun *jarrā* in the *Tahḏīb* (173), to which Ibn al-Sikkīt gives the meaning "messenger" (*rasūl*).

[63] Kopf, "Arabische Etymologien und Parallelen" (1958), 202.

[64] There is, for instance, a reference to a *hadīth* from Muhammad quoted in *Tahḏīb* (1. 364) which says "a *rajīᶜa* is something that returns to its original state." See also *Ṣiḥāḥ* 1. 466–67; *Qāmūs* 3. 68–69; *Lisān* 9. 471–73; *Maqāyīs* 2. 490–91; Lane, 1037–42.

Kopf's proposal appears to be based entirely upon data found in Dozy, which he has cited.[65] But there is really only one source that supports the meaning "become" and it is somewhat late and idiosyncratic: Idrīsī's *Glossaire Joint à la Description de l'Afrique et de l'Espagne*, published by Dozy and de Goeje in 1866. The title of this work alone suggests that it is concerned with usage primarily found on the fringes of the Arabic speaking world. And yet this single, relatively insignificant source is used by Kopf as the basis on which he constructs his theory of semantic development within this Arabic root.[66] This is far from persuasive evidence, particularly in view of the fact that in no other Arabic sources (including others that also reflect late usage from Spain and elsewhere) is there found a single indication that this proposed development from "return" to "become" has occurred.

3.2.5. SRR, *al-sirr* // *šārrekā*

The word *šārrekā* (Prov 3:8) has caused difficulties for translators who, after emendation, have usually rendered it as "your navel" or "your body, flesh." G. R. Driver believes a more proper translation is "your health" and argues for this on the basis of evidence from cognate languages, including this Arabic word.[67] Although the data from other languages might be useful in the defense of his position, the same cannot be said regarding Arabic.

There is no reference to health in any of the primary dictionaries consulted. The most basic meanings of the word are connected to joy, secrecy, the innermost part of a thing, and the furrows or lines on the face and forehead.[68] The only source that refers explicitly to health is Hava's dictionary which has the curious inclusion of "health, toast" after the usual and more expected mean-

[65] Dozy 1. 511.

[66] Dozy's citation of this source gives the impression that the verb is given the meaning "to become" in Idrīsī's work, but this is not true. This identification is actually made in a discussion of another root in Dozy and de Goeje's endnotes on Idrīsī's text. Two sources are cited which, they claim, support the translation "to become" for *rajaʿa*. These are both late sources which treat the Arabic of Spain and North Africa and only the relevant portion of their text is quoted and that out of context. It appears, however, that despite Dozy and de Goeje's claim otherwise the verb may still carry its usual sense of "return." There is, for example, their reference to the expression "this place has become (*rajaʿa*) a jungle" from Pedro de Alcala's early sixteenth century *Vocabulista Aravigo en Letra Castellana* which may just as easily be translated "this place has returned to being a jungle."

[67] G. R. Driver, "Problems in the Hebrew Text of Proverbs," 175.

[68] Lane, 1338; *Jamhara* 1, 81; *Ṣiḥāḥ* 1. 580; *Lisān* 6. 21–23 *Maqāyīs* 3. 67–69; other meanings found for the word include adultery/fornication (*Tahḏīb* 12. 284) and "vulva/penis"; these are clearly related to the idea of secrecy (*Qāmūs* 2. 48).

ings for the word. A glance further down the column in Hava reveals the origin of these meanings: there is an entry for the expression *bisirrika* that is translated "to your health."[69] This expression, however, is accompanied by the siglum indicating it is a modern Syrian form. It seems, then, that Driver has based his translation of the Arabic word on this one modern form found in Hava.[70] Furthermore, it should be noted that "to your health" is a free, idiomatic translation which is useless for getting at the authentic meaning(s) of the word. This, in itself, is enough to raise serious questions about the propriety of his proposal.

There is strong evidence to suggest that "health" may not be the most accurate translation of the Arabic word. The expression *bisirrika* is clearly in the form of a toast or wish directed toward another person. It could be, however, that by translating it as a reference to health Hava is simply capturing the general meaning of the expression in a way familiar to a Westerner without conveying its explicit meaning. This idea is supported by looking at the larger context of the root and its other possible meanings. As mentioned above, a very common meaning of the verbal form is "to be joyous, happy" and several nominal forms refer to the happiness and joy a person experiences. Even more striking are several other meanings for Driver's word (*sirr*): some sources refer to it as meaning "goodness, excellence."[71] Given this semantic context, then, it is more likely that the toast which Hava quotes is a wish or plea for lasting friendship and not specifically for the health of a person. The fact that health is not mentioned anywhere else in regard to the root clearly points in this direction.[72]

As mentioned above, this criticism does not totally negate the validity of Driver's proposal. It could be that the data he cites from other cognate lan-

[69] Hava, 316. It should be noted that Wehr does not include this meaning in his dictionary. Wahrmund (1, 891) says this expression is short for the fuller *bisirri maḥabattika*.

[70] I say "it seems" because Driver has not cited a single supporting source for "health" as the meaning of the word. He simply states that the word has this sense, giving the impression that this is common usage and well attested. This is something Driver does fairly frequently in his work. He regularly offers definitions for Arabic words without any mention of their sources or without indicating how these meanings might be related to other possible meanings of the word or root. In this way, the reader must either accept Driver's data with no questions asked or begin a sometimes extensive hunt for the material cited. This is clearly a serious methodological flaw that should be avoided when working with the Arabic sources.

[71] Lane, 1337–38.

[72] It should be noted that expressions conveying a wish for the health of another person are an important part of Arabic discourse. These typically contain words related to the root *ṣaḥḥa* in which the notion of physical health plays an important role. In modern Egyptian, for example, a very common idiom which expresses this sense is *ṣiḥḥitak* ("your health").

guages might support his reading of the Hebrew word. The intention here is to show that the Arabic evidence he cites is of no value to his theory. It is a misreading of a dictionary entry and disregard for the idiomatic nature of the translation.[73]

3.2.6. FRṬ I, *faraṭa, yafruṭu // pereṭ*

The word *pereṭ* in Lev 19:10 refers to the fallen grapes of the vineyard that the Israelites are not to gather but leave for the poor and strangers among them. The etymology of this word is uncertain, but Guillaume believes that the above Arabic verb and its meaning "to shake nuts from a tree" is related to it.[74] There are some problems with this suggestion. We should note from the outset that this sense of the Arabic verb does not comfortably fit the context of Lev 19:10. The reference there seems to be to grapes that have fallen naturally off the vine that are not to be picked up from the ground. The Arabic verb, on the other hand, points more in the direction of intentional removal of its produce from the tree through deliberate shaking of its branches.

This semantic difference aside, there is a more serious difficulty with this proposal. Doubts begin to surface immediately when we see that Guillaume has included the specification "Syrian" in parentheses after the meaning. This alerts us to the possibility that this may be a modern sense of the verb, and examination of the dictionaries indicates that this is indeed the case. Although he has not cited it, Hava appears to be Guillaume's source since it has the same meaning word for word and designates it with the symbol for the Syrian dialect. Similarly, Wehr contains the meaning "to strip off fruit" among several other possibilities.[75]

The belief that this is a modern meaning is verified by the older dictionaries which do not contain a single reference to fruits, nuts or the shaking of trees. In fact, there is nothing in the earlier sources that clearly explains the origin of this later meaning. Only two things suggest a possible connection between the primary meanings and this subsequent development. The most fundamental meaning of the Arabic root is "to go to extremes, outdo, surprise," as well as the practically opposite "to neglect." Another sense found frequently in the sources seems to be related to the idea of haste and hurrying, since there are

[73] *HALAT* 1522–23 labels this proposal by Driver as "very questionable."

[74] Guillaume, *Hebrew and Arabic Lexicography*, 4. 11.

[75] Hava, 556–57; Wehr, 706. See also Dozy 2. 255, which cites two modern sources to support the translation "to pick from the bunch" (*égrener*) for the first verbal form.

numerous references to acting hastily and quickly.[76] It is possible that the action of shaking a tree may be tied in with this sense of haste and stresses the inability to wait until nature takes its course and the fruit falls in its own time. Related to this is a meaning found primarily in the fourth form of the verb (*ʾafraṭa*), which describes the death of a young child before he or she has reached puberty. Once again, the theme of haste is present here and the act of forcefully removing its produce from the tree before it has fully ripened may be linked to early death.[77] Beyond these two senses there is nothing else that can be plausibly associated with the meaning that Guillaume has cited. His proposal is based upon one extremely late meaning for the Arabic verb that appears to support his conclusion.

3.2.7. KSF, *al-kasfatu // kōsep*

In a very clear example of scholarly nearsightedness, G. R. Driver refers to this Arabic word, to which he gives the meaning "disappointment, frustration," as being perfectly reflected in the Hebrew word *kōsep* which one manuscript adds to the end of Eccl 5:16.[78] Driver says the word "will here have the same sense" as the Egyptian Arabic word *al-kasfatu* and he cites Spiro's Arabic-English dictionary of the Egyptian dialect as his source.[79] In this way he has totally disregarded the historical development of this root as it is found in the primary Arabic dictionaries and isolated one very recent meaning found in only one section of the Arabic speaking world. To claim this as irrefutable evidence of the Hebrew word's meaning is clearly not very convincing.

The truth of the matter is that this Arabic word does not appear in any of the older dictionaries consulted and meanings having to do with frustration or disappointment are not found in any of the derived forms of the root. The Arabic

[76] See, for example the quote from al-Laith in *Tahḏīb* 13. 333, in which he refers to *ifrāṭ* as "something done hastily." Note also the treatments of the root in *Ṣiḥāḥ* 2. 235–36; *Jamhara* 2. 370; *Qāmūs* 2. 391; *Tāj* 5. 195–97; *Maqāyīs* 4. 490–91.

[77] If this idea of haste is the proper one in which to contextualize Guillaume's meaning this makes even more pronounced the semantic difference with Lev 19:10 mentioned above. The passage refers to the community's practice during harvest, at which time the produce of the land has already achieved maturation. There would therefore be no need to attempt to anticipate or speed up the natural processes.

[78] G. R. Driver, "Problems and Solutions," *VT* 4 (1954) 229.

[79] See S. Spiro, *An Arabic-English Dictionary of the Colloquial Arabic of Egypt* (Beirut: Librairie du Liban, 1973), where the word is given the meanings "sharp reply, rebuff, refusal of a favor, disappointment" (579).

verb *kasafa* means "to hamstring" or "to eclipse." While one cannot dismiss out of hand the possibility that the meaning "to cover, eclipse" (hence, to sadden) relates in some way to the Hebrew form and Driver's proposed meaning, this is not clearly found in the sources.[80] This example highlights in an extreme way the need to avoid reliance on modern sources and forms in working with the Arabic data. Any effort that does not consider such factors as the primary meanings of roots and the moment at which a particular form enters the Arabic language will inevitably be distorted and inaccurate in its interpretation.[81]

3.2.8. KLM, *al-kalimatu // maklîm*

The Arabic dictionaries are united in giving the sense "word, speech" or something related to this as the basic meaning of this nominal form.[82] It is therefore somewhat unusual that A. A. MacIntosh proposes the meaning "authority" and offers it as a cognate which can help interpret the word *maklîm* found in Judg 18:7.[83] He cites Dozy as his source for this translation, but it is quite clear that he has taken some liberties in how he has interpreted Dozy's data.

[80] Perhaps the closest sense is that of one's fate or luck turning bad. For instance, the expression *kasafa ʾamalahu* refers to a situation in which one's hope has been cut off and one is not happy (*Tahḏīb* 10. 76). But there is nothing in the dictionaries that directly supports Driver's meanings "disappointment, frustration." See, for example, *Maqāyīs* 5. 177–78. This is also the case for Wehr and other dictionaries of modern usage.

[81] A further indication of the danger of relying upon modern forms and meanings as supporting evidence is seen in Driver's treatment of the same root elsewhere. In his "Supposed Arabisms in the Old Testament," 101, he bases an LXX translation on the first form of the verb (*kasafa*), which he translates "to rebuke." He does not cite a source for this meaning, but study of the dictionaries suggests that it could only have been gotten from Hava, where it is clearly designated as a meaning that is unique to the modern Syrian dialect. Through such indiscriminate use of his sources Driver has proposed two different meanings for the same Arabic root, neither of which can be adequately supported by an appeal to the earliest dictionaries.

[82] See, for example, *Jamhara* 3. 169; *Ṣiḥāḥ* 2. 406; *Tahḏīb* 10. 264–65; *Qāmūs* 4. 174; *Lisān* 15. 427–29. Ibn Fāris, in his *Maqāyīs* (5. 131), says a second basic meaning of the root is that of "wound, injury."

[83] A. A. MacIntosh, "The Meaning of *MKLYM* in Judges XVIII 7," *VT* 35 (1985) 68–76. The textual problems with this verse, and in particular this portion of it, are substantial and a comparison of modern translations highlights the lack of agreement regarding how to solve them: "lacking nothing that is in the earth" (*NRSV*), "with no hereditary king to keep the country under his thumb" (*NEB*), "with no lack of any natural resources" (*NAB*), "there was no magistrate in the land that might put them to shame in anything" (*KJV*), "there was no lack or shortage of any sort in the territory" (*NJB*).

It must first be noted that the word "authority" never appears in any of the Dozy entries to which MacIntosh refers.[84] The meanings Dozy assigns to the form are *réputation* and *domination*.[85] MacIntosh acknowledges this but chooses to give the word the single meaning "authority" and translates it accordingly, even when he is directly quoting texts contained in Dozy. It therefore appears that he has ignored the diversity Dozy notes in the meaning of the form and given it a blanket meaning which better serves his purposes and supports his proposal.

Equally disturbing is the fact that MacIntosh has failed to mention the extremely secondary and late nature of the meanings he cites from Dozy. He gives the impression that these are meanings that are well attested in the Arabic sources though this is clearly not the case. There is no reference at all in the Arabic dictionaries to authority as a meaning of this form even in the sense of authoritative word or speech. There are only three sources Dozy refers to which are the basis of his meanings *réputation* and *domination*. One is a work on Mauritania edited by Tornberg in 1846, the second is another work edited by Dozy in the mid-nineteenth century and the third is the *History of the Berbers* by the famous Arab historian Ibn Khaldūn (1332-1406). It is clear that each of these is a source that reflects later usage of a small geographic area and cannot be used to make general statements about the meaning of a particular form, as MacIntosh has done, unless they can be supported by older and more authoritative sources.[86]

A final point on MacIntosh's treatment of this word touches on a critical point of methodology. In one of his footnotes he mentions that the root under discussion is only given a superficial analysis in Lane's Supplement. He then expresses appreciation to a colleague who has consulted the *Lisān* for him and has offered advice on the Arabic evidence. In effect, MacIntosh acknowledges his limitations in working with the Arabic data and his dependence upon

[84] Obviously, the word *kalimatun* ("word") also means the "say" one has in a matter, and this can logically translate into authority, but two factors work against such a development to support MacIntosh's suggestion. First of all, as will be seen below, the meaning "authority" is only found in a very limited portion of the Arabic sources. Secondly, it cannot be adequately demonstrated that the Hebrew root partakes of the meaning "to say."

[85] Dozy 2. 486.

[86] It is telling that the only source MacIntosh is able to quote which clearly gives the meaning "authority, influence, powerful position" is Wehr's dictionary (838). One cannot help but wonder if this were not MacIntosh's starting point and once he had discovered this meaning which supports an interesting reading of the Hebrew word in Judges 18 he then went about the task of trying to find it in earlier Arabic sources.

works written in languages other than Arabic (Lane, Dozy and Wehr) and other scholars who are able to work directly with the Arabic sources. This is a situation that is shared by most biblical scholars. Their limited knowledge of Arabic does not allow them to work directly with dictionaries written solely in Arabic, which usually give a fuller picture of a word's meaning and its place in the language. They are consequently always on the outside looking in and must rely upon works that are often incomplete or on other scholars whose analysis of the data may be less than thorough. Very often this type of approach results in the type of work of which MacIntosh's article is a prime example: a study which bases its conclusion on an inaccurate reading of only a portion of the data.

3.2.9. HBL, *al-habalatu // hebel*

Guillaume cites this Arabic word as a cognate form that supports the meaning "vapor, breath" for the Hebrew word *hebel*, which can have that meaning and also convey the figurative sense "vanity."[87] But the fact that this noun is not found in any of the primary dictionaries, including the extremely thorough and comprehensive *Tāj*, raises serious doubts about his proposal. Indeed, none of the other verbal or nominal forms under the root appear to make any reference to vapor or have anything to do with this sense.[88]

It is apparent that Guillaume is guilty of lexical myopia in this instance. Dozy is acknowledged as the basis of his translation, but Dozy cites only one late source with this meaning: Humbert's guide to conversational Arabic.[89] Other dictionaries that reflect modern usage also classify it as a recent form and meaning. Hava, for instance, contains the word *habalatun* and designates it as being from the modern Syrian dialect. In the same way, Hava lists as Syrian any other derived forms that refer to vapor.[90]

This is far from compelling evidence to support Guillaume's suggestion. The absence of this meaning in the earliest sources urges caution against seeing it as a basic part of the root's semantic field. It is even conceivable that the influence between Arabic and Hebrew in this case may have run in the

[87] Guillaume, *Hebrew and Arabic Lexicography* 1. 8.

[88] *Ṣiḥāḥ* 2. 628; *Tahḏīb* 6. 307; *Tāj* 8. 162–63. According to the *Maqāyīs* (6. 30–31), the root has three primary semantic bases: bereavement, heaviness, and deception.

[89] Dozy 2. 745.

[90] Hava, 813–14. The second and fifth verbal forms are given the meanings "to give a vapour bath" and "to take a vapour bath" respectively. See also Wehr (1017), which contains the same meaning for the fifth form in modern literary Arabic. Wahrmund (2. 1094) lists the meaning of the form *hablatun* as "steam (bath)" with the sign for neologism.

opposite direction. Perhaps the presence of this meaning in Hebrew led to its introduction into the Arabic root.[91]

3.2.10. YMM, *al-yamm // yēmim*

The word *yēmim* of Gen 36:24 has presented problems for translators and G. R. Driver notes that renderings such as "mules" and "hot springs," both of which appear in certain translations, are unsatisfactory on philological and/or contextual grounds. He prefers the translation "marsh fish" and bases his suggestion on the Arabic word cited.[92] When we turn to the Arabic dictionaries for verification of this, it is clear that his proposal cannot be sustained.

He cites Dozy as the basis for this translation but here we again encounter a meaning that is attested in a source that is relatively useless for the light it can shed on the Arabic data. This time, however, there is an interesting variation on the theme. Rather than citing Arabic evidence Dozy refers to the *Thesaurus Syriacus*, edited by R. Payne Smith in the latter part of the nineteenth century, which contains a cognate Syriac word that means a type of marsh fish weighing a pound or a pound and one half.[93] Although there may be a connection between the Syriac and Arabic words on the level of orthography, there is nothing in the Arabic sources that can be used to defend the notion that the similarity extends to the sense/semantic level. It is quite apparent that the primary meaning of the Arabic word is related to the sea and there are no references in the dictionaries to fish of any kind.[94] In an unusual example of lexical myopia Driver has latched onto this one reference in Dozy in an attempt to offer a creative reading of a troubling biblical Hebrew word. By basing his suggestion solely on evidence from Syriac, while ostensibly appealing to Arabic, Driver has virtually ignored all of the Arabic data related to the word. He has had to do this for a very obvious reason: there is nothing in the Arabic vocabulary to support his position.[95]

[91] *HALAT* (227) is also guilty of seeing a connection between the Hebrew word and this Arabic form, which it transcribes *habalat* and translates as "vapor" (*Dampf*). This is presumably based either on Hava's dictionary or Guillaume's proposal.

[92] G. R. Driver, "Genesis XXXVI 24: Mules or Fishes," *VT* 25 (1975). 110.

[93] Dozy 2, 854. The actual meaning given in J. Payne Smith is "a kind of lake fish." See J. Payne Smith, *A Compendious Syriac Dictionary founded on Thesaurus Syriacus of R. Payne Smith* (1st ed.; Oxford: Clarendon, 1903) 193.

[94] *Ṣiḥāḥ* 2. 724; *Qāmūs* 4. 195; *Tāj* 9. 114–15. The same is true for J. Payne Smith's Syriac dictionary where a large number of references to the sea are found under this root.

[95] The only animal that is reliably connected with the Arabic root *ymm* is a type of dove.

In this chapter we have tried to identify and illustrate a type of lexical myopia that often characterizes the work of biblical scholars who consult the Arabic data in their study of biblical Hebrew lexicography. The primary methodological flaw they all share is an inability to extend their horizon of vision back far enough to include the material contained in the earliest and most comprehensive Arabic sources. Consequently, their sight stops short at a particular temporal or geographic point along the line of development that is sometimes many centuries removed from these early dictionaries. In each case, therefore, the Arabic data cited has really nothing to say regarding the biblical forms that are studied. In order for an Arabic word or meaning to have even some relevance for and applicability to biblical Hebrew lexicography it is essential that it be attested in these earliest sources, which were themselves composed centuries after the biblical texts.

A final point is related to what was said at the beginning of this chapter about the lack of knowledge of Arabic on the part of some scholars being a major reason why they must rely upon dictionaries that give meanings in a western language. A listing of the scholars discussed most frequently in this chapter indicates that this is certainly not the case here. The majority of examples we have analyzed come from the pens of G. R. Driver, Guillaume and Kopf, who are all sufficiently competent in Arabic to be able to refer to sources in the original language. Yet we have seen that they, too, occasionally fall victim to lexical myopia and base their proposals on data that are late and/or dialectal. The reasons for their doing this undoubtedly vary, but their inattentiveness is quite unfortunate. They know better and should have done all they could to prevent this from happening in their work because of the message it sends to other scholars. Driver's (or another Arabist's) regular reliance upon Hava or Dozy as the basis for his conclusions suggests that it is perfectly legitimate for another scholar with little or no familiarity with Arabic to do the same. This chapter has highlighted the disastrous results this can have for biblical Hebrew lexicography.

CHAPTER 4

Elaborating/Confusing the Semantic Development: Astigmatism

The two previous chapters have attempted to identify the existence of two different types of errors. The guiding motif chosen to categorize these errors has been borrowed from language related to sight. "Tunnel vision" and "myopia," terms that describe defects in the ability to see, pointed to certain general tendencies occasionally found in the proposals of scholars making use of Arabic in biblical Hebrew lexicography. This visual terminology seems appropriate since the difficulties typically encountered are problems of vision. For one reason or another, the examples studied so far have all been found to be wanting due to the inability of the scholars proposing them to accurately see the Arabic evidence in its proper context. In the case of tunnel vision, it is the wide context that is missed, while with myopia the deep context is ignored.

We now turn to a third type of oversight that is perhaps most aptly termed astigmatism. This oversight is marked by an inability to focus clearly on the evidence as it is presented in the sources, which then leads to a distorted perception of the data and the advancement of suggestions that have no genuine basis. At first glance, this seems to be the same problem encountered in the two previous chapters, but that is not really the case. In the examples seen thus far, there has always been some evidence, no matter how slight, from the Arabic sources which supports the scholars' claims. The scholars' problem has been one of selectivity and exclusivity as they have focussed too narrowly on one very limited portion of data found in the Arabic dictionaries.

Lexical astigmatism is something entirely different. Scholars who fall victim to this condition do not base their conclusions on any solid evidence found in the sources. Because of their inability to focus clearly, their proposals are founded upon a completely distorted view of the evidence, or, in some extreme cases, evidence that is nonexistent and the consequence of their own astigmatic condition. The difference between this and the two previous types of errors should be apparent: while tunnel vision and myopia ignore some part of the context, astigmatism misreads the entire context.

Three different types of lexical astigmatism can be distinguished. Although these are clearly related phenomena, each is concerned with a specific form of the problem. Of particular interest is the language in which the misreading occurs. In some cases there is a lack of focus regarding the Arabic side of the Arabic/Hebrew equation, and in others the blurred vision is found on the Hebrew side. In keeping with the focus of this study, primary attention will be given to the Arabic side. But some examples on the Hebrew side will also be cited so as to better illustrate the nature of the problem. The major characteristics of these three types can be summarized in the following way.

1) Going Beyond the Arabic Evidence

Sometimes a scholar will totally misread the Arabic data found in the dictionaries and thereby construct a case on nonexistent evidence. A common way in which this occurs is through improper extension of a well attested meaning wherein the scholar introduces a new meaning into an Arabic word or root that is then taken as a proper development of a more basic sense that *is* clearly found in the sources. This interpolates an unattested meaning into the semantic discussion. Other forms of this problem are more extreme and include the fabrication of an entirely new Arabic root or meaning that has no suitable foundation. This baseless Arabic form or meaning is then introduced into Hebrew lexicography and proposed as the solution to a problem in Hebrew.

2) Using Arabic To Go Beyond the Hebrew Evidence

Problems of a different type are found in proposals where the lack of lexical focus exists in the scholar's application of Arabic evidence in the interpretation of biblical Hebrew. In these cases, the Arabic data may be well documented and properly analyzed, with the difficulty arising in the application of the scholar's conclusions to Hebrew. A major issue here is the question of the legitimacy of introducing meanings and forms found within a root in a related language into the linguistic realm of a perceived cognate root in a different language. For example, semantic developments which are clearly found in Arabic may be applied to related Hebrew forms even when there is no evidence for such a development within Hebrew. Elsewhere, Arabic may be used to emend an apparently sound Hebrew word and put it under a new root. Here, too, some rather extreme forms of astigmatism can be found. On occasion, by emendation entirely new Hebrew roots are created whose existence is argued for as a type of "mirror form" reflecting a well attested root in Arabic.

3) Comparing Etymologically Unrelated Forms

A third type of misuse is found in those proposals which take a known semantic development in Arabic and impose it on a lexically unrelated Hebrew word with which it shares a meaning. In this way, a false equivalence is set up between two different forms in Hebrew and Arabic in which data from one (usually Arabic) are improperly introduced into the semantic range of the other.

An important difference between the second and third types of error and the first one discussed is that while those in the first category are clearly always wrong because they are based on a misreading of the Arabic evidence, errors of the second and third types are not *a priori* wrong since the Arabic evidence has usually been properly interpreted. The difficulty with these latter cases arises in determining whether or not a parallel development has taken place in Hebrew. It is possible that such a development may have occurred that is not reflected in the biblical text, but since an argument based on conjecture is difficult to prove, this type of proposal must be greeted cautiously.

The proposals we will now consider are examples of this lexical astigmatism. Each proposal suffers from the same symptoms: an inability to focus properly on the data which leads to blurred vision and a misreading of either the Arabic or Hebrew context.

1) Going Beyond the Arabic Evidence

4.1.1. BRZ I, *baraza, yabruzu // pĕrāzôn*

P. C. Craigie argues that this Arabic verb, which he translates "to go forth into battle," furnishes the meaning of the word *pĕrāzôn* in Judg 5:7, which he then translates "warriors."[1] The curious identification of the first sounds in the Arabic and Hebrew roots (Hebrew *pe* = Arabic *fāʾ*) is an initial difficulty which the author attempts to address, and which is a major obstacle to his proposal, but our main interest is in his use of the Arabic data. This is a clear case of reading more into the Arabic data than one should and thereby constructing an argument on evidence that does not really exist.

Craigie is not quite correct in saying that this Arabic verb can mean "to go forth into battle," for this usage is only possible when the battle or war is explicitly stated, as in the expression found in Lane *baraza ʾilā l-qirni fī l-ḥarb* ("he stepped forward to meet his adversary [lit. "his match"] in battle"). The basic sense of the verb is simply "to protrude, emerge, appear," and the form by itself does not carry any militaristic connotation whatsoever.[2] In other words, without a direct reference to a combative context the Arabic verb alone refers to nothing more than coming forth and becoming prominent. Furthermore, although the larger context of the Deborah story is obviously militaristic, this is not true for the verse in question. This is seen, for example, in the *NRSV*, which gives the term *pĕrāzôn* the meaning "peasantry" and translates the verse "The peasantry prospered in Israel, they grew fat on plunder, because you arose, Deborah, arose as a mother in Israel."

This proposal appears to be a case of *petitio principii* ("begging the question"). The author wants to justify the following "grew fat on plunder" and needs to turn the peasants into warriors. Thus he forces the evidence to fit his purpose. It therefore seems that Craigie is seriously misinterpreting the Arabic evidence by introducing a sense into the root that is not normally a part of it unless it is explicitly indicated in the context. It is therefore inappropriate to introduce this same sense into the Hebrew word. If he must appeal to this Arabic root to propose a meaning – which, as said above, is highly questionable from the point of view of phonetic equivalence – a more proper translation might be "those who come forth."[3]

4.1.2. Tʿ I, *taʿataʿa // yitʿû*

This same Arabic verb was studied in the previous chapter with reference to Guillaume postulating a Hebrew reading on the basis of its meaning "to pull a

[1] P. C. Craigie, "Some Further Notes on the Song of Deborah," *VT* 22 (1972) 350.

[2] Lane, 186. See also *Jamhara* 1. 254; *Tahḏīb* 13. 201; *Tāj* 4. 5–7; *Maqāyīs* 1. 218. The primary sense of emergence is seen in the nominal form *birāz* ("excrement").

[3] The treatment of this root in *HALAT* (908) is most unsatisfactory. It lists Arabic *faraza* as a suggested cognate form and then cites Craigie's proposal in connection with this Arabic root rather than *baraza*. This creates the false impression that Craigie's suggestion is based on an Arabic form that is etymologically related to the Hebrew word.

tooth." Here we treat G. R. Driver's reference to it with the meanings "to stutter," "to be indistinct" to help explicate the word *yitʿû* in Job 38:41.[4] The subject of the Hebrew verb is young ravens, and Driver believes it is "hardly possible" (contrary to the *NRSV*, *JPS* and *NAB* translations) to apply the usual sense of "wander" to them, so he proposes to find a more fitting meaning by appealing to Arabic data.

Driver suggests that the Hebrew verb actually refers to the twittering or croaking of the young ravens and bases this on the above Arabic verb which, according to him, derives its basic meaning from an onomatopoetic reiteration of light sound. He has clearly read too much into this Arabic root and has introduced a sense which does not derive from authentic Arabic sources. As seen in the last chapter, the meaning "to stutter" under this root appears to be related to that of pulling a beast from soft earth, as both actions attempt to "get out" something which is "stuck." There is no reference in the sources to either the onomatopoeia or the reiteration of light sounds that Driver detects.[5] These characteristics are simply not found within the use of this root. He has, in short, proposed a semantic development in the Arabic form that is not attested in the Arabic sources and then applied it to a perceived Hebrew cognate.

4.1.3. ṮĠR, *al-ṯaġr* // *šaʿar*

Guillaume appeals to this Arabic form to give the first word of the construct phrase *šaʿărê ṣalmāwet* in Job 38:17 the meaning "boundaries" and then translates the phrase "the confines of darkness."[6] He believes the first use of the word *šaʿărê*, found earlier in the verse, preserves its usual meaning of "gates" and this second mention of the same word with a different meaning is an example of homonymy in biblical Hebrew. Although such homonymy is well attested and known to be a feature of biblical Hebrew, the Arabic sources cannot be used to defend its existence here.

Senses related to confinement and boundaries are not a part of this Arabic word's semantic range. In fact, there is strong evidence to suggest that the opposite meaning is more basic. A very common meaning is that of a gap between teeth, a breach in a wall or some other opening which rather provides access to the other side than prevents it. Another frequent sense is that of a

[4] G. R. Driver, "Problems in Job," 167–68.

[5] Lane, 307.

[6] Guillaume, "The Arabic Background of the Book of Job," *Promise and Fulfillment* (ed. F. F. Bruce; Edinbourgh: T. & T. Clark, 1963) 123–24.

point on the frontier which gives access to a land and from which an invasion of the enemy is expected and feared. During the period of Arab conquests certain frontier towns were called *ṯuġur*. It can be a place like a mountain pass or even a fortress through which the enemy may pass due to some imperfection in construction.[7] Given this evidence, Guillaume's translation "boundary" relies on a very superficial reading of the dictionary entry and on the interpretation of "frontier" in the sense of "confinement." The boundaries that are spoken of under this root do not confine but allow easy passage from one side to the other. The Arabic evidence cannot be cited in support of a sense "confines."

4.1.4. ṮLM I, *ṯalama, yaṯlimu* // *hišlîm*

In a clear case of trying to stretch the semantic range of a root to its breaking point and thereby reading too much into the Arabic evidence, G. R. Driver cites the above Arabic verb as support for his reading of the phrase *miyyôm ʿad-laylâ tašlîmēnî* (*NRSV* – "from day to night you bring me to an end") in Isa 38:12,13 as "from day until night you torment me."[8]

The most common meanings within the Arabic root are related to the theme of breaking. Usually it refers to a break in something solid that then leads to a gap or a hole in it. For instance, common verbal meanings have to do with breaking or denting the edge of a sword, a vessel, a wall or a trench so that it now contains breaches, dents or gaps. Similarly, nominal forms refer to the gap or breach of a thing that is broken. This meaning can also be used in a metaphorical sense as in the following quote found in the *Tāj*: "The death of such a one is a gap (*ṯulma*) in the body of Islam, a gap that will not be filled up."[9]

Nowhere in the sources is there a reference to Driver's meaning "to afflict, torment." It might be reasonable to suggest that once something has a hole in it it is ruined and therefore a source of affliction for the one(s) to whom it belongs, but even this possible semantic development – not cited in the dictionaries – does not have the sense of complete and ongoing torment which Driver claims is being expressed by the Hebrew phrase.[10]

[7] *Ṣiḥāḥ* 1. 155–56; *Qāmūs* 1. 397; *Tahḏīb* 8. 88–89.; *Tāj* 3. 75–76; *Maqāyīs* 1. 378–79; Lane, 338–39.

[8] G. R. Driver, "Isaiah I–XXXIX," 56.

[9] Quoted in Lane, 350; see also *Jamhara* 2. 49; *Qāmūs* 4. 87; *Tahḏīb* 15. 92–93; *Lisān* 14. 345–46; *Maqāyīs* 1. 384.

[10] His insistence on this being the primary sense of the word is seen in his rejection of the common translation of it ("to make an end of") because this is a momentary action that cannot

The suggested sense "to afflict, torment" is not a part of the Arabic root's semantic field. We see this clearly when we study a citation within the root in which there is a direct reference to human persons: the expression *ṯulima fī mālihi* means "he suffered the loss of some of his property (or money)." A portion of the individual's possessions is now gone but the emphasis is not on the person's troubled and afflicted state of mind. The stress, rather, is on the the fact that *some* of it has been removed while much of it still remains. Once again, the idea of gaps and holes is central and appears to be the basic idea here.

Driver has illegitimately extended the meaning of this Arabic verb to support what he believes is a more accurate translation of the Hebrew cognate. This root is concerned with the phenomenon of the breakage or partial removal of parts of an object that is seen as a unified entity be it a wall, sword, trench or one's accumulated possessions. Because it is not interested in what one's reaction to this breakup might be and gives no indication that the result is unmitigated disaster, Driver's statement that the Arabic verb conveys a sense of affliction or torment is erroneous.

4.1.5. ḤṢṢ I, *ḥaṣṣa, yaḥuṣṣu // ḥōṣēṣ*

In order to support his claim that the word *ḥōṣēṣ* suggests that the locusts in Prov 30:27 (*NRSV*—"The locusts have no king, yet all of them march in rank") are marching in organized formation, D. Winton Thomas appeals to this Arabic verb, which he translates "to mass together."[11] He maintains that the meanings of the verb in its third and fourth forms ("divided with a person," "gave a share to") and its sixth form ("divided between each other"), as well as the nominal form *ḥiṣṣa* ("portion, share") suggest the massing of the locusts in ordered divisions. This is unfairly stretching the well established meaning of the Arabic forms which, in fact, seems to point in the opposite direction from the one proposed by Thomas.

The most common meanings found within this Arabic root have to do with division and separation, not unification and coming together.[12] This is clearly

be repeated from day until night as the verse states. But this apparent failure to take into account the poetic nature of the text and the fact that each word does not have to be interpreted literally is not our concern.

[11] D. W. Thomas, "Notes on Some Passages in the Book of Proverbs," *VT* 15 (1965) 276–77.

[12] See, for example, *Qāmūs* 2. 309–10, which gives the meaning "to divide" for the second verbal form, and *Jamhara* 1. 60–61, *Tahḏīb* 3. 401, and *Tāj* 4. 379–81 which all give "to divide" as a meaning for the third form of the verb. *HALAT* (330) also identifies division and separation as the primary sense of the Arabic verb.

seen in the frequent references in the dictionaries to the verb's describing the loss of hair from the head due to shaving, cutting, rubbing, or disease.[13] The sense of "portion, share" highlights the same thing – the stress is on the individual as distinct and apart from the group, not on the corporate identity or group reality. The Arabic sources say nothing about massing together in an orderly fashion, but only speak of a division that leads to separation and isolation.

Thomas has proposed a semantic development within this Arabic root that is not reflected in the dictionaries. He claims the root describes a type of division which leads to the neatly arranged order of a military formation, but there is no evidence of this in the sources since they speak primarily of fragmentation and disintegration. It appears that he has done this to point out the usefulness of the Arabic data in determining how variant readings have developed. According to Thomas, the texts of some of the versions suggest the idea of "massing together," and he contends that this same meaning can be obtained from Arabic *ḥaṣṣa*. Our analysis has shown that this contention is unwarranted and misleading.

4.1.6. RBW I, *rabā, yarbū// ribbîtî*

Because he believes the word prior to it (*ṭippaḥtî*) in Lam 2:22 refers to physical growth and development, G. R. Driver maintains that the verbal form *ribbîtî* in the same verse expresses the notion of the mental and spiritual growth of a child and enlists this Arabic cognate for support.[14] This interpretation is challenged by the Arabic evidence since it is quite clear that in the earliest sources the root is concerned only with physical maturation and that there is no reference to mental or spiritual development.

The verbal forms can refer to the growth or physical enlargement of something animate or inanimate. It is common to speak of the fostering, cultivation or nourishment of children, trees, plants and vegetables. A good example of such usage is seen in the *Qurʾān* (22:5) where Allah says "You see the lifeless

[13] There are many examples of both verbal and nominal forms describing this phenomenon in Lane. There are three main semantic bases of this root according to the *Maqāyīs* (2. 12–13): portion/share, the clarity/appearance of something, and lessening/diminishing.

[14] G. R. Driver, "Hebrew Notes on 'Song of Songs' and 'Lamentations'," *Festschrift für Alfred Bertholet* (ed. Walter Baumgartner et al.; Tübingen: J. C. B. Mohr, 1950) 138–39. The *NRSV* translation of the relevant portion of the verse reads "those whom I bore and reared my enemy has destroyed."

earth; but when We send water down upon it it stirs, swells (*rabat*) and grows every type of beautiful vegetation." In the same way, inanimate objects can also be referred to, as in expressions which speak of the augmentation of one's property and wealth as a result of usury. In no place where a human being is the referent, however, does the growth or development described take on an intellectual or spiritual sense. It is always used in the context of physical feeding, fostering or rearing.[15]

It appears, then, that Driver has shifted the focus of this Arabic root significantly by introducing into it the sense of mental and spiritual growth of a child. Since the Arabic sources make clear that the rearing and raising of children is an important part of the root's semantic range this would not be an illogical or unreasonable extension of meaning. In fact, the later development of the Arabic language will follow this very route, as seen in the common use of the verb in modern literary Arabic to refer to instruction, education and teaching.[16]

However, since the mental/spiritual aspect of child raising is not cited in the older Arabic dictionaries which stress only the physical dimension, it is proper to question the validity of Driver's proposal and its applicability to biblical Hebrew. In this instance, the proposed semantic development does in fact take place in rather later Arabic usage, but that does not provide evidence to support such a development in a much earlier period.

4.1.7. SJW I, *sajā, yasjū* // *šāgû*

G. R. Driver cites this Arabic verb and its meaning "to be wrapped up" as the basis for his translation of the phrase *wĕgam ʾēlleh bayyayin šāgû* (*NRSV* – "These also reel with wine.") in Isa 28:7 as "these too are addicted to wine."[17] He suggests that the image of being wrapped up mirrors the experience of the

[15] *Ṣiḥāḥ* 1. 461–62; *Tahḏīb* 15. 272–76; *Qāmūs* 4. 333–34; *Tāj* 10. 142–43; *Maqāyīs* 2. 483–84.

[16] See, for example, the references to education and the like in Wehr (324). This step from physical to mental growth is an easy and logical one and could occur independently in every language. Therefore, neither is evidence from Arabic needed, nor is lack of same an argument against it. The main question should be: does the Hebrew context call for such a variation?

[17] G. R. Driver, "'Another Little Drink' – Isaiah 28:1–22," *Words and Meanings: Essays Presented to David Winton Thomas* (ed. P. Ackroyd & B. Lindars; Cambridge: University Press, 1968) 51–52. Note that Driver's reading was accepted into the *NEB* translation. The revision of the *NEB*, the *REB*, however, gives the translation "These also lose their way with wine."

addict who is hopelessly caught up in his or her obsession and he then introduces this meaning into the Hebrew cognate.

This proposal is riddled with difficulties, not the least of which is the very nature of the semantic leap Driver proposes from being wrapped in a shroud or blanket to the tormenting experience of drug or alcohol addiction. It may be granted that the addict's situation can be likened to that of being trapped in a web from which one cannot escape, and this is a variation on the theme of being wrapped up, but there is nothing in the Arabic sources that suggests Arabic usage made such a connection. Indeed, an examination of the Arabic data suggests that the primary mood of this root is far from the terrifying and frantic tone that Driver's translation implies.

As Driver himself notes, one of the basic meanings of the verb in its first form refers to the night as its darkness extends and all becomes silent, quiet and still. This is seen in the short verse from the *Qurʾān* (93:2) "And by the night when its darkness spreads out (*sajā*)." It can also be used to refer to the wind and the sea as they become calm or still. The link between these meanings and that of being wrapped up is clear: the change from light to darkness in the case of the night and from storm to quiet in the case of the wind and sea is a shift that produces a feeling of silence that comes over one as a type of cover that surrounds all things. Peace and quiet is the predominant image here and this is nicely captured in what may be the most common covering action mentioned in the sources: the act of wrapping the corpse in the winding sheet in preparation for burial.[18]

In this semantic context Driver's meaning "to be addicted" is out of place. He has probably interpreted the sense of being wrapped up in negative terms as an experience of being caught up in a net and hopelessly out of control. From such a perspective the idea of addiction makes sense. But our analysis has shown that this is not the way the Arabic sources define this root. They see it in a much more positive light. It refers to the cover of peace and quiet that is found over the earth as darkness descends or which is felt in the air and over the sea after the storm has passed. Driver has not considered this semantic context of the root and in so ignoring it has introduced a foreign element into it which he has erroneously applied to Hebrew.

[18] Properly speaking, the meaning "cover" exists only in the second verbal form. *Ṣiḥāḥ* 1. 569 refers to the wrapping of the dead person as well as other meanings emphasizing rest and quiet. Cf. *Tahḏīb* 11. 140–41, *Lisān* 19. 91–93, and *Maqāyīs* 3. 137 . The important role rest and peacefulness play in this root can also be seen in the frequency with which words based on the root *sakana* ("to rest") appear in the entries treating *sajā* in the dictionaries.

4.1.8. SᶜL I, *saᶜila, yasᶜalu // neᶜĕlāsâ*

The Hebrew verb *neᶜĕlāsâ* of Job 39:13 has the wing of the ostrich as its subject and the form has caused some difficulty for translators and commentators. G. R. Driver sees an example of metathesis here and believes this Arabic verb, which he translates "to be mean, paltry, little," is a useful cognate which suggests the sense "atrophied" for the Hebrew word. He then translates the first part of the verse as "is the wing of the hen-ostrich atrophied?"[19]

This is another example of a misuse of the Arabic material which draws more out of the evidence than the data are able to supply. But before we examine how Driver has done this we must first point out the inaccurate citation of the Arabic. Although a verb exists with these three root letters, it does not ever convey the meaning "to be mean, paltry, little." Rather, when it is vocalized in this way it carries the sense "to be brisk, lively, sprightly."[20] This cannot possibly be the basis for Driver's translation. The puzzle is solved when we posit a typographical or proofreading error and change the initial root letter from a *sīn* to a *ṣād* and the verb becomes *ṣaᶜila* which, although it still requires quite a semantic leap, is closer to Driver's meaning than the form he cites. It appears, then, that the word has been improperly transcribed through the omission of the dot under the first letter, thereby inadvertently referring to an entirely different word.[21]

The verb *ṣaᶜila*, while closer to the meaning Driver gives, is hardly a perfect equivalence. It can refer to being slender or small, but when describing humans or animals it is always with regard to those that are small in the head and long in the neck. It is also used frequently to describe a palm tree that is very tall.[22] There is some suggestion in the sources that it can refer to being slight of build in general, but the stress is always on the head in relation to the rest of the body. Most interesting for our purposes is the fact that the only animal consistently cited in the Arabic sources is the ostrich, which is the animal mentioned in the verse under discussion. But it is clear that it is the

[19] G. R. Driver, "Birds in the Old Testament II," 138, n.2.

[20] See, for example *Qāmūs* 3. 406–07; *Tāj* 7. 375; Lane, 1365. When it is vocalized as *saᶜala*, with a *fatḥa* over the second root letter, it carries meanings related to coughing.

[21] As is frequently the case elsewhere, Driver does not give any sources or references for this verb and its meaning in his text. This makes it impossible to know with certainty if the scenario just described is in fact what happened. All things considered, it appears to make the most sense and offers the simplest explanation. This situation highlights the importance of consistent and accurate citation of all forms and sources when working with the Arabic data.

[22] *Tahḏīb* 2. 33–34; *Tāj* 7. 403; Lane, 1690–91.

shape of the bird with its long, slender neck and relatively small head that is the point of reference and that its lower body and wings never enter into the discussion. Furthermore, there is no support in the Arabic dictionaries for Driver's sense of "atrophy." The head is not small because it is shrinking or diminishing in some way. This is simply the way things are as the verb describes a continual state or condition.

We have here another clear case of *petitio principii*. Driver is pressing hard because he must have seen somewhere that the verb *ṣaʿila* has a specific relation to ostriches and means "having a thin neck and small head." Thus, it "had to be" connected with the ostrich passage in Job.

By appearing to base his translation "atrophy" on the Arabic verb *ṣaʿila* Driver has interpolated a sense into the root that is foreign to it. He has taken the legitimate meaning "to be small (in the head)" and reshaped it in such a way that it now describes a process rather than a state and this is then applied to a different part of the bird's anatomy. This runs counter to all the data found in the Arabic sources and is an unconvincing attempt to argue for a new translation of the Hebrew. It also presumes an unwarranted metathesis and an irregular correspondence between *samekh* and *ṣād*.

4.1.9. ʿLQ I, *ʿaliqa, yaʿlaqu // ʿălûqâ*

In an attempt to explicate the troublesome word *ʿălûqâ* (Prov 30:15) J. J. Gluck proposes the translation "erotic passion" and relies heavily upon this Arabic verb and the meanings "to cause to burn," "to love physically" to defend his choice.[23] Most modern editions translate the word as "leech," but frequently note its problematic nature. This meaning is well attested in the cognate Arabic form *ʿalaq* ("leech") which is clearly connected to the primary sense of the root of clinging or attaching to something. "To love" is also a part of this Arabic root's semantic range, and the dictionaries explicitly state that this is also related to the idea of attachment. The *Tahḏīb*, for example, says the verb can mean "to love" due to the fact of one's heart being attached to the beloved.[24]

[23] J. J. Gluck, "Proverbs XXX 15a," *VT* 14 (1964) 367–72.

[24] *Tahḏīb* 1. 244; see also *Ṣiḥāḥ* 2. 148–49, *Lisān* 12. 133–34, and *Maqāyīs* 4. 125 which also explicitly speak of the uniting of one heart to another as the focus of the verb when it refers to love. Another meaning for the verb that is frequent is "to conceive" and its presence seems to support Gluck's analysis of the root and the importance of physical love within it. But closer examination challenges this. The word *ʿalaq* also means "blood clot," and whether this is due to its connection with the leech or because it sticks and coagulates is difficult to say. It is important to

Gluck has expanded on this idea of love somewhat and given it a more carnal interpretation with his translation "erotic passion." This cannot be supported by the Arabic sources since each time love is referred to it is the emotional dimension and not the physical aspect or expression of it that is discussed.[25] Gluck has tried to underline this sense of passionate, erotic desire by citing two other meanings for the verb: to cause to burn and to love physically. As we have seen, the latter of these is not really found in the Arabic sources. He has probably based this meaning on that of "to conceive" which is found within the root. But this is an improper extension of meaning since the sources clearly indicate that it is, once again, the sense of attachment and not that of physical love that is the basis for the meaning "to conceive."[26] In the same way, the meaning "to cause to burn" which seemingly supports Gluck's "erotic passion" is actually useless for his discussion since it is limited to modern Syrian usage and is not attested in any of the earliest dictionaries.[27]

It appears that Gluck has based his proposal regarding this difficult Hebrew word on evidence that is not really there. He suggests an improper nuance of the legitimate meaning "to love" by extending the sense in a way the data do not support. The semantic development he believes has occurred within the root that leads to his meaning "erotic passion" has not actually taken place but is the result of a faulty reading of the data.[28]

---

note in this connection that according to ancient belief conception is the result of a fusion between the sperm and a blood clot in the womb (apparently misunderstood menstruation). The *Qurʾān* (96:3) says "He created you from a blood clot." Thus, it is more likely that the verbal meaning "to conceive" is denominative and secondary to "blood clot" and has nothing to do with "to cling." This further damages Gluck's proposal.

[25] This can be seen in the treatment of the root in Lane, 2132–38, which consistently refers in a more indeterminate way to the emotional aspect of love and does not support Gluck's reading "erotic passion." It should also be noted that while meanings related to love are very well attested in this Arabic root they are clearly secondary and subordinate to the more basic one of attachment discussed above.

[26] See, for example, the reference in Lane (2133) that speaks of the metaphorical use of the verb to describe a plant growing and changing in the earth as it develops in much the same way the fetus does in the womb.

[27] See Hava, 494. There is a touch of irony in this since Gluck initially dismisses the meaning "leech" for the word because he has found no evidence that this animal was used for medicinal purposes in the ancient world. Here, he cites for support a meaning which cannot be found in the ancient sources.

[28] For another treatment of Gluck's proposal that comes to the same conclusion as the one here see F. S. North, "The Four Insatiables," *VT* 15 (1965) 281–82. It should be noted that *HALAT* (786) cites Gluck's proposal, but also refers to several other attempts to understand the Hebrew term that are based on Arabic words related to "leech" and "demon."

4.1.10. FDD I, *fadda, yafiddu // pāzaz*

Guillaume again takes special liberties with his phonemic equivalences in his suggestion that this Arabic verb, which he translates "to be alone, apart," is somehow related to the Hebrew root *pāzaz*.[29] This Hebrew verb, usually taken as meaning "to be refined," is found only in 1 Kgs 10:18, where it appears in the masculine singular participial form of the Hophal conjugation. The identification of Arabic *dāl* with Hebrew *zayin* cannot be defended, which creates initial problems for Guillaume's claim that there is a connection between these two roots. Of interest here, however, is his disregard for the evidence of the Arabic dictionaries and his seeming fabrication of a new meaning for the word.

The Arabic sources all agree in seeing the primary meaning of this root as connected to the idea of raising the voice and crying out. In a sense that is related, reference is also sometimes made to walking or treading upon the earth in a proud or forceful manner.[30] There is no mention of any meaning connected to Guillaume's sense "to be alone, apart." He appears either to have found it in an obscure source or, in another example of *petitio principii*, to have generated it to support his theory.[31] Whatever its origin, it is unsubstantiated by the authoritative sources and therefore cannot be seen as a legitimate part of the root's semantic field. Guillaume has clearly introduced it in a way that can only be termed a misuse of the Arabic data in working with biblical Hebrew.

2) Using Arabic To Go Beyond the Hebrew Evidence

4.2.1. ʾSR I, *ʾasara, yaʾsiru // ʾāsar*

The Hebrew root *ʾāsar* is usually found with the meaning "to bind, imprison," and this meaning is also a basic part of the semantic range of its

[29] Guillaume, *Hebrew and Arabic Lexicography*, 1. 13.

[30] See, for example, *Tahḏīb* 14. 73–74. where Ṯaʿalab says it refers to a man walking on the face of the earth in pride and strength. The *Tahḏīb* also says it can describe the sound of men raising their voices as they work hard during plowing. Similar meanings are found in *Ṣiḥāḥ* 2. 228, *Qāmūs* 1. 333–34, *Tāj* 2. 448–49, *Maqāyīs* 4. 438, and Lane, 2350–51.

[31] Guillaume acknowledges the dubious nature of his proposal by adding a question mark after the Arabic form he cites but he does not explain what this signifies – is he questioning the form or the meaning? It is possible that his suggestion may be based on dialectal Arabic. Some areas (especially Iraq) reduce the word *fard* ("individual") to *fad* and use it practically as an indefinite article "a, one." Guillaume may have picked this up somewhere and, not knowing the true story of its development, used it for his purpose.

Arabic cognate *ʾsr*. But the latter root can also at times carry the sense of massing together, as in certain texts which speak of divine creation as a bringing together of the various joints and parts of the body into one whole.[32] Connected to this idea are Arabic meanings that refer to an individual, thing or group in its entirety or togetherness. For example, a very common expression in Arabic uses the prepositional phrase *biʾasrihi* to denote the totality of something as in *al-qawmu biʾasrihim* ("the people in its entirety," "the people altogether"). Another clearly related form is *ʾusra*, with the meaning "family." There is an obvious close semantic connection between such meanings and the basic one of "to bind or tie together," and it appears that the meaning of the Arabic root has developed from an original notion of binding an animal or prisoner to include the massing together of individual members or elements into a unified whole.

On the basis of this Arabic data G. R. Driver argues for the existence of a similar semantic range in the Hebrew root. He proposes that the words *ʾussārû* and *ʾussĕrû* mean "was compacted together, huddled together" and says that the text of Isa 22:3, rather than speaking of people being bound or taken prisoner, refers to their huddling together in groups.[33]

This is a clear example of a misuse of the Arabic sources which is not due to an inaccurate reading or interpretation of them but is a result of the misleading application of one's findings. Everything Driver states about the Arabic root is correct and factual. It does have these several different meanings, although he does not explicate the semantic connection that unites them. Problems begin to surface, however, when he tries to relate the Arabic data to biblical Hebrew. As mentioned above, the root *ʾāsar* unquestionably shares the meaning "to bind, make prisoner" with Arabic *ʾsr*. However, there is no direct evidence that the Hebrew root extends this meaning in the way the Arabic does to include any reference to creation or the joining together of individual elements into a single unity. The sole semantic context for the Hebrew root, when used either literally or metaphorically, is that of tying up or binding someone or something in order to limit mobility or prevent escape.

It appears, then, that Driver has read something into the biblical Hebrew lexicon that is not there. He notes an extended meaning in the Arabic cognate and then imposes it onto its Hebrew counterpart. But there is no basis for argu-

[32] Examples of such expressions are found in Lane, 57–58; see also *Ṣiḥāḥ* 1. 25; *Jamhara* 3. 249; *Tahḏīb* 13. 60–2; *Lisān* 5. 76–78; *Maqāyīs* 1. 107.

[33] G. R. Driver, "Isaiah I–XXXIX," 47.

ing the existence of this meaning in Hebrew other than Driver's claim that the translation he quotes ("they were bound by the archers" — *RV*) is "absurd."[34]

4.2.2. ṮFL I, *ṯafila, yaṯfulu // šāpēl*

G. R. Driver considers the usual translation of Isa 32:19, describing the downfall of the forest and the city being laid low, to be at odds with a context that presents a picture of idyllic peace. He therefore proposes a different translation which highlights the presence of several homonymous roots he detects within the verse. One such root is *šāpēl*, found twice in the second half of the verse, which Driver translates the second time not with its usual sense "to be humiliated, laid low" but "to laze," thereby depicting a scene of peaceful relaxation ("the city will laze in the lowlands").[35]

This proposal is based on the Arabic evidence he cites regarding the root *ṯfl*, which he claims means "to subside" in the first verbal form, "sat and talked with (a person)" in the third form, and "(a man of lazy disposition) shirks great deeds" in the fifth form. He therefore sees an element of laziness as a consistent theme throughout the Arabic root which then justifies translating its Hebrew cognate in the same way. Driver has committed a double error with this proposal since he has both seriously misinterpreted the Arabic data and on that basis introduced a sense into the Hebrew root that cannot be supported.

The evidence for translating the first verbal form as "to subside" is far from compelling. Lane notes that it does carry this meaning in the dictionary of Golius but he has not found it in any other lexicon, including the *Ṣiḥāḥ* which Golius cites as his basis for this translation.[36] This sense is probably connected with the nominal form *ṯufl* which refers to the dregs, sediment or settlings of something. Even if "subside" can be plausibly argued as a meaning within this root it is still quite a semantic jump to Driver's meaning "to laze." The dictionaries are unanimous in the lack of any meanings related to this sense.[37] This

[34] The one version which adopts Driver's proposal is, not surprisingly, the *NEB*: "Your commanders are all in flight, huddled together out of bowshot; all your stoutest warriors huddled together, they have taken to their heels." The *REB* keeps this same general sense: "All your commanders are in full flight; fleeing in groups from the bow; all your stoutest warriors dispersed in groups have fled in all directions."

[35] G. R. Driver, "Isaiah I–XXXIX," 52–53.

[36] Lane, 340.

[37] See the treatments found in *Ṣiḥāḥ* (1. 156), where the nominal form refers to the dregs that no one else wants and *Jamhara* (2. 48), which adds that it could also refer to excrement; see also

is clear when we observe the lengths Driver must go to in order to stretch accepted meanings to give him the sense he wishes.

His translation of the third derived form (*ṯāfala*) as "sat and talked with (a person)" is a case in point. According to Lane, a more probable translation is "to eat (dregs or grain)" or "to eat with another." The meaning "to sit and speak with" is, according to the *Tāj* and the *Qāmūs,* based on a statement by one ancient witness, Ibn ʿAbbād, who says that *ṯāfala* means the same thing as *ṯāfana* ("to sit with another, fighting or consulting"). This suggests that the focus of this form of the verb is simply on sharing the grain or gruel at the bottom of the pot. Speaking is only by implication.

We see the same type of doctoring of data in Driver's use of the fifth verbal form *taṯaffala,* which he translates "(a man of lazy disposition) shirks great deeds." His use of parenthetical cue cards to include material not found in the dictionaries in order to guide the reader's interpretation alerts us to Driver's editorial presence. Even his use of the word "shirks" implies a certain willful and malicious intent to not get the job done which is not found in the Arabic sources. The general sense of this form is of some quality preventing someone from generous action. According to Lane the cause of this is some character flaw that is basic to the individual's personality. Its exact nature is not stated and is perhaps purposely left vague so as to cover a wide range of possibilities. Driver has specified it more than the evidence allows in order to support his contention that laziness is an important part of this root's semantic field. This is a very misleading statement.[38]

The double nature of Driver's error should now be apparent. He has improperly introduced a false sense into the Arabic and then extended it to the Hebrew. As we have seen, there is no textual justification for his opinion that the theme of laziness is found within the Arabic root *ṯfl.*[39] This fact alone makes it wrong for him to then argue for the meaning's existence within the Hebrew root *šāpēl.* Beyond this, however, is the question of how legitimate it is to introduce even well attested Arabic meanings into Hebrew roots which do not contain them. If the Arabic sources better supported Driver's proposal

---

Tahḏīb 15. 90–91 and *Tāj* 7. 244–45. Probably the closest we come to a meaning that can be related to laziness are several references to the form *ṯafāl* which carries the sense of "slowness" and can describe a camel that will not get up and move unless it is prodded.

[38] Wahrmund (1. 382) supports the translation "to weigh down and thus prevent, be a dead weight upon someone" for the fifth verbal from. This goes with "dregs" and can be used figuratively.

[39] According to the *Maqāyīs* (1. 380) all meanings under this root can be traced back to the primary one of "to be settled down under something."

would it then be acceptable? Given the lack of any meanings remotely related to laziness under this Hebrew root, this question must be answered in the negative. Furthermore, the passage does not cry out for some new interpretation. Despite Driver's protestations, the primary sense of the Hebrew word ("to lay low, humiliate") fits the context well.

3) Comparing Etymologically Unrelated Forms

4.3.1. RWᶜ I, *rāᶜa, yarūᶜu* // *rāhab*

A rather different instance of a type of problem in comparative lexicography is illustrated by Kopf's treatment of the Hebrew root *rāhab* on the basis of Arabic *rwᶜ*.[40] Since he recognizes that the roots are not etymological correspondents, Kopf's proposal might best be termed an exercise in comparative semantics.

Kopf notes that the Arabic root contains meanings that revolve around two different senses: one having to do with fear and surprise, and the other related to notions of pleasure and arousal.[41] He believes that the latter sense can help shed light on the true meaning of the Hebrew forms *rāhĕbām* (Ps 90:10) and *tarhibēnî* (Ps 138:3). Since, in his opinion, their usual interpretations related to pride go against their contexts, he prefers a sense related to pleasure and delight.

Kopf supports this sense by observing that in the *Hiphil* conjugation the root *rāhab* can carry the meaning "to make uneasy, frighten," while acknowledging that usage elsewhere suggests the root conveys other senses in other conjugations and forms. This encourages him to explore other avenues in an effort to discern precisely what those other meanings might be. Next, he notes the existence of the two meanings within the Arabic verb *rāᶜa*, one of which ("to frighten") is shared by *rāhab*. From here he simply introduces the other Arabic meaning ("to please, arouse") into the Hebrew root, presumably because a semantic link has been established with it by virtue of the fact that they both share the first meaning. He is quite explicit in his contention that the

[40] Kopf, "Arabische Etymologien und Parallelen" (1959), 273–76. He gives the word the sense "anything that makes you open your mouth or takes away your breath in fear or amazement."

[41] The Arabic dictionaries are clear on the presence of both of these senses. However, the *Tahḏīb* (8. 388) quotes a saying from al-Laith, referring to a nominal form, that points out the close semantic connection between the two meanings: "it is everything that makes you fear because of its beauty or abundance." See also *Ṣiḥāḥ* 1. 522; *Lisān* 9. 494–96; Lane, 1187–89. The *Maqāyīs* (2. 459–60), on the other hand, considers meanings related to fear to be the only legitimate ones.

semantic configuration found in Arabic is also present in Hebrew ("Eine ähnliche Bewandtnis muss es auch mit dem hebr. rāhab haben.") but never explains why this must be so.

Kopf has introduced a semantic twist into this Hebrew root with no internal or external support. Internally, there is no evidence at all that *rāhab* ever carries the sense of "pleasure" in any of its forms.[42] Externally, there is no reason why these roots should be seen as semantically related in a way that one can be used to interpret the other.[43] Kopf's only defense in doing this appears to be the common meaning ("to frighten") that they conditionally share. But this is extremely faulty methodology at work. The fact that two etymologically unrelated roots in two different languages share a specific meaning does not give one the right to ingenuously impose the entire semantic range of one of them upon the other as Kopf has done. One can imagine the disaster that would ensue were this acceptable practice! Kopf's error lies in how he applies the Arabic evidence rather than in how he reads it, but the end result for biblical Hebrew lexicography is the same.[44]

4.3.2. NHY VIII, *intahā, yantahī (ilā) // tam ʾel*

Kopf proposes that the Hebrew root *tam*, which typically carries the sense of completion or perfection, can also at times mean "to reach, acquire" when it is found in close proximity to the preposition *ʾel*. The phrase *ʾim-tam hakkesep ûmiqnēh habbĕhēmâ ʾel-ʾădōnî* (Gen 47:18) is identified as a case in point.[45] These words come from the Egyptians after the first year of Joseph's agrarian policy and are usually seen as two separate clauses and translated

[42] Conversely, there are no indications in the Arabic dictionaries that *ruʿ* ever carries the attested Hebrew meanings of pride and arrogance. This further weakens Kopf's semantic linking of the two roots.

[43] In principle it is legitimate to consider similar semantic developments in related languages, but the elements must be truly comparable. These two words are not. The verb *rāhab* means "to fear," while Arabic *rāʿa* means "to frighten." That you can make the first one mean the same as the second through the use of a causative is not enough to establish the equation Kopf sees between them. For recent studies of comparative semantics between Hebrew and Spanish see L. Alonso Schökel: "Hebreo + Español: Notas de Semántica Comparada I," *Sef* 47 (1987) 245–254; "Hebreo + Español: Notas de Semántica Comparada II," *Sef* 49 (1989) 11–19; "Hebreo + Español: Notas de Semántica Comparada III," *Sef* 54 (1994) 3–12.

[44] In logic this is known as the undistributed middle: horses have eyes; birds have eyes; therefore horses are birds. It is perhaps telling that *HALAT* (1112–13), in treating this Hebrew root, refers to Kopf's study, but only mentions his comments on the common meaning it shares with Arabic *rahiba* ("to frighten"). It contains nothing on his proposal based on Arabic *rāʿa*.

[45] Kopf, "Arabische Etymologien und Parallelen" (1959), 284.

along the lines of "our money is all spent; and the herds of cattle are my lord's" (*NRSV*). But Kopf believes that it should be seen as one complete phrase and chooses to translate it "the money and the cattle are (completely) in the hand of my lord" ("das Geld and das Vieh (vollkommen) in die Hand meines Herrn gelangt sind"). He bases this proposal upon the Arabic verb *intahā* which he says is synonymous with *tam*. Because *intahā* can mean "to reach, attain" when followed by the preposition *ilā*, Kopf concludes the Hebrew root *tam* can convey the same sense here since it precedes the preposition *ʾel*.

There are some serious flaws with Kopf's approach that involve both his interpretation of the Arabic data and his application of it to biblical Hebrew. In the first place, Kopf is mistaken in his statement that *tam* and *intahā* are synonymous. *Intahā* is the eighth verbal form of the Arabic root *nahā* and, while it may carry meanings that are related to completion and perfection, it can also refer to abstaining or refraining from something because it is forbidden.[46] Its semantic field is therefore broader than that of the Hebrew root and it is inaccurate to simply equate the two as synonyms. It also appears that Kopf has improperly extended the meaning of the Arabic phrase *intahā ilā* to better fit the biblical Hebrew context. This phrase typically describes situations that speak in abstract terms of a person attaining things like authority and fame or of news and information finally reaching a person. It does not normally refer to concrete items like the money and cattle mentioned in Gen 47:18. The Arabic phrase, consequently, does not appear to fit comfortably into the context of the passage and its value as a cognate form has been exaggerated by Kopf.

But we do have a clear cognate form that is synonymous in the Arabic root *tamma*. It shares the same primary sense of completion or perfection with *tam* and the meanings of many of its derived forms have echoes in the Hebrew root.[47] This appears to be a more logical place to look for assistance from Arabic in uncovering the meaning of its Hebrew counterpart. The drawback of this approach for Kopf is that the Arabic root does not really add anything new to the discussion since its semantic field mirrors closely that of *tam*. For a parallel semantic field for his proposed sense, Kopf has to look beyond

[46] The clearest examples of meanings related to completion are seen in those which speak of something ending or a thing/affair attaining its utmost possible degree or point. See, for example, Lane, 3039.

[47] Lane, 315–17. In Arabic *tamma* and *intahā* are not synonyms. The former means "to be completed," the latter "to come to an end." Their contents may coincide, and this leads to the confusion of the treatment here. If a book is completed it is also at its end, but if an activity ends it is not necessarily complete.

tamma to find evidence that could support a different lexical interpretation of the Hebrew word. That is, in order to expand a Hebrew root's semantic range he simply introduces data from an etymologically unrelated root in Arabic. The semantic range of an Arabic form with a similar meaning, at least in part, is thus used to expand the possible understanding of a biblical text.

4.3.3. WRY I, *wariya, yarī// bārāʾ*

In a rather surprising example, J. R. Busto Saiz claims that the above Arabic verb with its meaning "to be fat, healthy" can be helpful in uncovering the true meaning of the word *bôrĕʾêkā* ("your Creator") in the phrase found in Eccl 12:1 *ûzĕkōr ʾet-bôrĕʾêkā bîmê bĕḥûrōtêkā* ("Remember your Creator in the days of your youth."). On the basis of forms such as *bārîʾ*, "fat," Busto Saiz posits a second root *bārāʾ* which, unlike its better attested homonym which means "to create," conveys the sense of "being fat." He then uses the Arabic data to extend that meaning and suggests that "health" is the proper sense of the word in Eccl 12:1. He translates the verse accordingly: "Remember your good health in the days of your youth."[48]

This proposal is riddled with difficulties. From the phonological point of view, the equivalence of Arabic *wāw* and Hebrew *beth* makes no sense.[49] He does argue well and convincingly that the interchange of the final *yōd* and *ʾālep* can be supported in post-biblical Hebrew and that it therefore does not present a major obstacle. But the alleged equivalence of the two initial radicals defies explanation since it is virtually impossible to argue that an Arabic root beginning with a *wāw* and a Hebrew one beginning with a *bêt* are cognate forms, yet this is precisely what he has done. In fact, his entire argument hinges on this identification since the idea of "health" which is the basis of his proposal is something that is, according to Busto Saiz, found only on the Arabic side of the equation. The Hebrew forms he cites speak only of becoming fat. It appears, therefore, that this example is similar to the two previous ones from Kopf since Busto Saiz proposes a comparison between two etymologically unrelated roots in Hebrew and Arabic.

[48] J. R. Busto Saiz, "בוראיך (Qoh. 12,1), reconsiderado," *Sef* 46 (1986) 85–87.

[49] I initially thought the suggestion that *wariya* is somehow related to *bārāʾ* had to be a typographical error for a root with a *bāʾ* as the initial letter. But after searching the Arabic dictionaries under all possible alternatives, including *bariya*, *bariʾa*, and *barā* and turning up nothing while, at the same time, discovering some very slight evidence to support Busto Saiz's verb as written (see below), I now conclude that no mistake was made.

Bracketing for a moment the dubiousness of his argument on purely phonological grounds, we encounter a significant problem when we examine the Arabic data. Busto Saiz lists several meanings for the verb *wariya*, including "to heal, cure," "to be healthy," "to be fat," and "to be strong," and there is a clear semantic connection among them all. But the only one of these which is clearly present in the sources is "to be fat," and it typically refers to a camel or some other animal.[50] It appears, then, that Busto Saiz has painted an inaccurate picture of this root's meaning in order to give the impression that healthiness is a significant theme within it. He then compounds his error by introducing this improper sense into the Hebrew data. Note how much more serious Busto Saiz's mistake is than Kopf's. Kopf's reading of the Arabic evidence is accurate and the semantic development he notes has, in fact, taken place. The same is not true for Busto Saiz, who has proposed a development that cannot be supported. Despite this difference between the two, however, they share a common flaw: a method that seeks to exchange data between two etymologically unrelated roots that cannot be easily linked semantically.[51]

In this chapter we have attempted to document the existence of a type of linguistic astigmatism which occasionally characterizes the work of biblical scholars who make use of the Arabic data. The shared shortcoming of all of these examples is their inability to properly focus upon and interpret the overall linguistic context. Because of the blurred vision which these scholars experience they misread the Arabic evidence. Their motivation often seems to be their wish to prove a preconceived idea.

Our documentation and study of three different forms such astigmatism can take – going beyond the Arabic evidence, using Arabic to go beyond the Hebrew evidence, and comparing etymologically unrelated forms – has suggested that such errors are typically the result of very idiosyncratic readings of the data which produce puzzling proposals.

This highlights a problem which we did not encounter when we discussed tunnel vision and myopia. In those two categories of misuse we are usually able to pinpoint a precise reason for the mistake and identify some concrete cause for the error. Although we may not agree with the proposal, the conclusion it reaches is usually understandable in light of the methodology used and the

[50] See, for example, *Ṣiḥāḥ* 2. 683, *Tahḏīb* 15. 308, and *Maqāyīs* 6. 104. Even here the meaning "to be fat" is a relatively secondary meaning within this root's semantic field.

[51] *HALAT* (147) cites the Arabic verb *wariya* ("to be very fat") as a cognate form but does not offer any support for this claim.

scholar's interpretation of the data studied. This is often not the case with astigmatism – it can defy explanation, although the subconsciously driving mechanism behind it may be identifiable as *petitio principii*. It is sometimes very difficult to see where the ideas and arguments that support the scholar's proposal have come from. Clear and tangible evidence of a lexical nature which has contributed to the process of arriving at a conclusion is often absent because the mistake is more one of misreading the entire context rather than misreading isolated portions of it. This makes it an error of a more frustrating and troubling type whose causes are harder to determine and understand.

Guidelines for the Use of Arabic in Biblical Hebrew Lexicography

Having concluded discussion of the three main types of errors found in the work of biblical scholars who appeal to the Arabic data and having examined in detail specific examples of each of these types of mistakes, we are now at a point where some guidelines for a proper method can be put forth based on the results of our study. The concern throughout has been with determining how best to effectively make use of the Arabic resources in biblical Hebrew lexicography and the following guidelines are proposed as the most reliable way of realizing that goal. They are presented under three headings which are chronologically listed, each treating a different stage of the scholar's method: distinguishing the sources, interpreting the evidence, and applying the results.

Distinguishing the Sources

1) Prefer Arabic-Arabic Dictionaries

Ideally, one should refer to sources in Arabic which offer a full historical discussion of forms and meanings. The *Lisān* and *Tāj* are highly recommended as comprehensive tools in this regard. The *Qāmūs* is less complete due to its tendency toward brevity but is still extremely useful. The *Tahḏīb* is also an important source to consult since it typically cites words in context from ancient authorities.

2) Consult Lane

Lane offers a viable alternative. The vast majority of Hebrew Bible scholars do not have the competence in Arabic necessary to consult the dictionaries mentioned above. As a *minimum,* however, one must refer to Lane since he usually presents a very accurate and accessible picture of the material found in the earlier Arabic sources. A major shortcoming of the work that must be kept in mind is the fact that the last two volumes are less complete than the others and must be used cautiously. Since all Arabic words in Lane are given in the original script with no transliteration, knowledge of the Arabic alphabet and the basic rules of morphology is essential to use the lexicon.

3) Supplement Dozy

Because it frequently contains examples of material from Arabic speaking Spain which is temporally and geographically limited Dozy must be used with caution. Some of its unique material may indeed be early and reflect ancient usage, but without any external controls or support this is very risky data upon which to base an argument. It is best to use Dozy in tandem with Lane or one of the Arabic language sources which can then verify its contents. Dozy also demands some basic knowledge of Arabic since it, too, only lists forms in the original script.

4) Avoid Modern Dictionaries

Texts like Belot, Hava, Bocthor, Wehr and a host of others should not be consulted as primary sources since they are typically concerned only with modern forms and meanings. Their primary purpose is to simply give a translation in a European language and they rarely discuss questions of a linguistic or historical nature which are essential to the determination of relevancy for biblical Hebrew. Although such resources may contain material that is ancient and relevant for biblical Hebrew, there is no way of knowing which data are useful and which are not without reference to a more comprehensive dictionary like Lane.

5) Do Not Rely on Biblical Hebrew Dictionaries

Resources like *HALAT* and BDB regularly list Arabic cognate forms and meanings in their entries for biblical Hebrew. Sometimes these are supported by references to scholarly works and sometimes they are not. These citations are not always trustworthy and should be carefully studied and verified.

6) Do Not Accept All Published Proposals As Correct

The appearance of a proposal in print does not automatically authenticate it. This is a common belief when reading the work of scholars like Driver and Guillaume whom even some Arabists see as "experts" in Arabic. A false conclusion is often perpetuated because it originally came from the pen of a perceived authority. Always confirm a suggestion put forth by someone else before accepting it.

Interpreting the Evidence

7) Distinguish The Semantic Range

It is essential to have a good understanding of the range of meanings found in the semantic field of a given root. Know which senses are more basic and primary and which may be later developments from these original meanings. This enables proper analysis of the data and categorization of evidence.

8) Focus On Well Attested Meanings

Do not base proposals on meanings that are rare or extremely secondary. The likelihood of the presence of an Arabic meaning in a related Hebrew form diminishes greatly when its existence in Arabic is very limited. In particular, do not suggest a reading that is found in only one relatively minor Arabic source but is missing in all of the important dictionaries. The greater the number of Arabic sources containing a meaning the more plausible the argument for its presence in Hebrew becomes.

9) Avoid Usage Limited To A Particular Time or Place

Forms and meanings that are regionally or temporally limited should be treated cautiously. Some of this material may be indicative of ancient usage, but, as we saw with guideline number three above, without any clear way of knowing what is relevant and what is not it is best not to base one's argument on such a shaky foundation. If support can be gotten from another, more reliable, source this can serve to validate the meaning. But without such external confirmation data of this type should not figure in discussions on the use of Arabic in biblical Hebrew lexicography.

10) Do Not Improperly Extend Meaning

It is essential to accept and work with the meanings which are found in the Arabic sources. There is a great temptation to extend and elaborate upon the extant meanings, but this is to be avoided. Even the most logical and natural of extensions cannot serve as the basis for a proposal if that precise meaning is not found in the Arabic dictionaries. What results in this case is a reading which has no precise basis and the question of its applicability to biblical Hebrew is therefore highly speculative.

Applying the Results

11) Follow The Rules of Lexical Equivalence

The laws governing the relationships between Arabic and Hebrew graphemes ("letters") are well established and should be known to all scholars engaged in comparative work. These rules are predictable and dependable and therefore should not be violated. It is important when offering proposals for biblical Hebrew based on Arabic that the equivalences between the Arabic and Hebrew forms be consistent with the rules. Even a difference of one grapheme/letter can put a form within an entirely different root and nullify the proposal. This guideline must be strictly followed because without it there are no controls on the process and one can defend proposals that break the rules by appeal to everything from metathesis to dialectal variation. For assistance in determining the equivalences consult the table in Appendix B.

12) Never Assume Parallel Semantic Development

If a semantic development has occurred within Arabic one cannot assume that it has also taken place in a related biblical Hebrew form. This is a particularly common error when two words share the same meaning. It is wrong to claim that a development of the meaning which is clearly attested in Arabic must have occurred within Hebrew even though there is no evidence for it. The development of meanings is unique to each language, takes place within a larger semantic field, and cannot be transferred from one language to another.

13) Never Impose Meaning On An Unrelated Form

This guideline is related to the previous one but refers to a more serious offense. One should not propose a comparison between two etymologically unrelated forms which share a meaning. If an Arabic word shares a meaning with an otherwise unrelated Hebrew word one cannot impose the entire semantic range of the Arabic word, or any portion of it, on the Hebrew word. The semantic history and range of each form is distinct and unique and should not be made to conform to another.

14) Do Not Anticipate Conclusions

One should never approach a problem of biblical Hebrew lexicography with a particular answer in mind. If one has a preconceived idea about what a Hebrew form means and is determined to find evidence from Arabic to support that conclusion the effort is doomed from the start. The Arabic evidence must be interpreted and applied on its own terms and any attempt to force the data to fit one's pre-formed conclusions or pet theory will usually lead to inaccurate results.

APPENDIX A

Examples of Proper Use of Arabic in Biblical Hebrew Lexicography

The purpose of the present work has been to identify and illustrate some of the most common types of errors found in the work of scholars who refer to the Arabic data in their discussions of biblical Hebrew forms. Consequently, it has been necessary to frequently adopt a negative or polemical tone in the analysis of their work and its value. But it is important to remember that such problematic scholarship does not characterize the vast majority of attempts that use the Arabic sources to illuminate the biblical text. Although enough examples of misuse exist to make necessary an appeal for a sounder methodology, most efforts have demonstrated careful and judicious use of Arabic. It therefore seems appropriate to briefly consider a few examples of contributions to the study of biblical Hebrew lexicography that are distinguished by the thoughtful attention they pay to the Arabic sources. Four recent examples of such work have been chosen and will be discussed.

1. ḤṢB I, *ḥaṣaba, yaḥṣibu // ḥōṣēb*

In an article on Ps 29:7 E. Greenstein challenges H. L. Ginsberg's assertion that appeal can be made to this Arabic verb to give the word *ḥōṣēb* in that verse the meaning "ignite."[1] Greenstein correctly observes that this proposal is based on a misunderstanding of the Arabic root. He makes good use of Lane's dictionary to point out the fact that any meaning related to fire is connected to the root's primary sense of throwing. The focus is not on the wood being

[1] E. L. Greenstein, "YHWH's Lightning in Psalm 29:7," *Maarav* 8 (1992) 52.

ignited by the flames, as Ginsberg wrongly interprets, but the action of tossing the wood on the fire. Greenstein also refers to the lexically related Arabic root *ḥṭb* to further support his position. In this way, he has demonstrated a fine understanding of the importance of interpreting the Arabic evidence within its proper semantic/lexical context in order to avoid a distorted reading of the data.[2]

2. RKB II, *rakkaba, yurakkibu // rākab*

Although it is not a treatment which bears directly on biblical Hebrew lexicography, V. Sasson's study of a word found in one of the Arad ostraca inscriptions is closely connected and worth mentioning due to his careful consideration of the Arabic cognate evidence.[3] He discusses and rejects the opinion concerning the word *trkb* found in inscription no. 1, first put forth by E. Ullendorff and later refined by S. P. Brock, that this Arabic verb supports the existence of the meaning "to gather, compose" for the root *rkb* in the Semitic languages.

The attentive nature of his analysis of the Arabic data is evident in several important ways. In the first place, Sasson carefully distinguishes among the different verbal conjugations that are used to support the proposal. He notes how the spelling and meaning can change depending upon whether one is referring to the first (*rakaba*), second (*rakkaba*), or sixth (*tarākaba*) verbal form. This is an issue that is too often ignored by biblical scholars but is crucial in determining the position of a particular form or meaning within the larger semantic range of a root. Secondly, he recognizes the critical role prepositions can play in extending meaning. The addition of a preposition can sometimes introduce a new semantic base for a root and this is very important for the Arabic form being considered here. He notes that its basic meaning is "to mount, ride" but when followed by the words *ʿala* ("upon") or *fī* ("in") it can take on the meanings "to put, place, mount something on" or "to fit, mount, insert something in," respectively. Sasson correctly refers to these as "secondary significations" since they are not found within the root proper but

[2] When scholars attempt to make use of Arabic in biblical Hebrew lexicography the concern most often is with offering new proposals for meanings. But this example illustrates another type of contribution which is equally important: studying and critiquing earlier proposals to determine their accuracy and usefulness. A huge body of material has accumulated over time and much of it, especially proposals that have been accepted by the scholarly community, needs to be evaluated. The four examples treated in this appendix all fall into this category of refutations of earlier proposals.

[3] V. Sasson, "The word *TRKB* in the Arad Ostracon," *VT* 30 (1980) 48–49.

introduced into it through the use of prepositions and he properly argues against using them to support the contention that the meaning "to gather, compose" is basic to this Arabic root. Finally, Sasson is also to be commended for pointing out the fact that some expressions using verbal forms built on the root *rkb* which are basic to Brock's position are more commonly found with words based on the root *rkm*. This raises some suspicions and introduces the possibility that such meanings may not have been part of the root *rkb* originally but are the result of dialectal variations or some other phenomenon. Attention of this kind to such often negelected details should be a part of all scholarly efforts to use the Arabic data.

3. RṢD I, *raṣada, yarṣudu // tĕraṣṣĕdûn*

A number of translations have been proposed for the word *tĕraṣṣĕdûn* in Ps 68:17 and J. A. Emerton considers several of them in an article that treats the previous verse.[4] Two of these proposals appeal to this Arabic verb for support and Emerton correctly argues against them because they are based on an improper interpretation of the Arabic data. The primary sense of the Arabic verb is "to watch, wait" and it often refers to waiting along the road for someone or some thing. As Emerton observes, at times this meaning has been either improperly extended or inaccurately applied to the Hebrew word in an attempt to understand it.

M. D. Cassuto has translated it as "to wait yearningly for the moment when one's time will come" based on this same meaning's existence within the Arabic root *rṣd*. But Emerton properly cautions "whether we should explain the Hebrew on the basis of what may be a special development in Arabic." Although he does not elaborate on the nature of this "special development" within Arabic, Emerton's point is well taken.[5] One should not simply transfer a meaning, particularly a rare or suspect one, from one language to another in order to solve a lexicographical problem.

Another common solution is to give the word the meaning "to watch with envy." As Emerton points out, this theory also originates in Arabic, where the

[4] J. A. Emerton, "The 'Mountain of God' in Psalm 68:19," *History and Traditions of Early Israel* (ed. A. Lemaire and B. Otzen; Leiden: E. J. Brill, 1993) 28–29. This is the only example of the Hebrew root *rāṣad* in the biblical text.

[5] In fact, the meaning "to wait yearningly for the moment when one's time will come" is not actually a part of this Arabic root's semantic range. The only time it carries this sense is when it is accompanied by other words which set this context. A good example of this is the expression "she watches, or waits, for the drinking of others, that she may drink" (*tarṣudu šurba ḡairiha litašraba hiya*) which is found in the *Qāmūs* and cited in Lane, 1092.

meaning "to watch" is clearly found, but it gives to the Hebrew verb a sense not attested in Arabic. A double violation has occurred here with both an improper extension of meaning to the Arabic verb and then its application to the Hebrew form. Emerton's analysis highlights well the pitfalls that one encounters when not carefully interpreting the Arabic data and his method serves as a fine example of how to avoid them.

4. WDᶜ I, *wadaᶜa, yadaᶜu // yādaᶜ*

Perhaps the most outstanding and comprehensive example of how to properly use Arabic in biblical Hebrew lexicography can be found in a recent study by W. Johnstone. In a carefully argued article Johnstone definitively proves that D. Winton Thomas' long held and often repeated opinion that Arabic supports the existence of a second form of the Hebrew root *yādaᶜ* cannot be sustained.[6] He does this through an examination of the Arabic dictionaries and argues that "in order to appreciate Arabic meaning in context one must turn to Arabic sources." Johnstone begins by critiquing Thomas' method and finds three areas of weakness in it. In the first place, he observes that Lane's lexicon, which is an important source for Thomas, is not a very reliable resource due to the fact that the discussion on the root *ydᶜ* is found in the very deficient latter part of the work. Secondly, Thomas' reliance on Hava is also challenged since it contains no examples of usage in context. Finally, he questions some of the liberties Thomas takes in his interpretation of the Arabic data as, for example, when he shifts from a passive to a stative form of the verb and when he adds explanatory remarks not found in the original sources.

He then refutes Thomas' findings point-by-point through appeal to three primary sources: *Qāmūs*, *Tāj*, and *Lisān*. Throughout this insightful discussion Johnstone demonstrates a flawless methodology and intimate knowledge of the sources he consults. He identifies three criteria he deems essential if one wishes to use Arabic in a philological argument: 1) the meanings of the words cited need to be verified by use in Arabic contexts; 2) the location of meanings within the evolution of sense within the Arabic root must be recognized; 3) the Arab account of morphology/etymology has to be considered. Any Hebrew bible scholar wishing to draw upon the data found in the Arabic sources will be guaranteed reliable results if Johnstone's method and message are followed.

[6] William Johnstone, "*YDᶜ* II, 'Be Humbled, Humiliated'?" *VT* 41 (1991) 49–62.

APPENDIX B

Lexical Equivalences between Hebrew and Arabic

HEBREW	ARABIC
א	*alif* (ʾ)
ב	*bāʾ* (b)
ג	*jīm* (j)
ד	*dāl* (d)
ה	*hāʾ* (h)
ו	*wāw* (w)
ז	*zāʾ* (z); *d̲āl* (d̲)
ח	*ḥāʾ* (ḥ); *k̲āʾ* (k̲)
ט	*ṭāʾ* (ṭ)
י	*yāʾ* (y)
כ	*kāf* (k)

ל	*lām* (l)
מ	*mīm* (m)
נ	*nūn* (n)
ס	*sīn* (s)
ע	*ʿain* (ʿ); *ġain* (ġ)
פ	*fāʾ* (f)
צ	*ṣād* (ṣ); *ḍād* (ḍ); *ẓāʾ* (ẓ)
ק	*qāf* (q)
ר	*rāʾ* (r)
שׁ	*šīn* (š)
שׂ	*ṯāʾ* (ṯ); *sīn* (s)
ת	*tāʾ* (t)

Bibliography

Albright, W. F. "Mitannian Maryannu 'Chariot Warrior' and the Canaanite and Egyptian Evidence." *AfO* 6 (1930–31) 217–21.

Alonso Schökel, L. "Hebreo + Español: Notas de Semántica Comparada I." *Sef* 47 (1987) 245–54.

________. "Hebreo + Español: Notas de Semántica Comparada II." *Sef* 49 (1989) 11–19.

________. "Hebreo + Español: Notas de Semántica Comparada III." *Sef* 54 (1994) 3–12.

al-Azharī. *Al-Tahḏīb fīl-Luġa.* 15 vols. Cairo: Dār al-Miṣrīya lil-Taʾlīf wal-Tarjama, 1964.

Barr, J. *Comparative Philology and the Text of the Old Testament.* Winona Lake, IN: Eisenbrauns, 1987.

Bergsträßer, G. *Einführung in die semitischen Sprachen.* Munich: M. Hueber, 1928.

Brown, F., S. R. Driver, and C. A. Briggs. *A Hebrew and English Lexicon of the Old Testament.* Oxford: Clarendon, 1952.

Calderone, P. J. "*ḤDL*-II in Poetic Texts." *CBQ* 23 (1961) 451–60.

Cohen, D. "La Lexicographie Comparée." *Quaderni di Semitistica* 2 (1973) 183–208.

Cohen, M. "Langues Chamito-Sémitiques." *Les Langues du Monde.* Ed. A. Meillet and M. Cohen. Paris: Centre National de la Recherche Scientifique, 1924, 81–181.

Craigie, P. C. "Some Further Notes on the Song of Deborah." *VT* 22 (1972) 349–52.

De Saussure, F. *Cours de Linguistique Générale*. Paris: Payot, 1916.

Dozy, R. P. A. *Supplément aux Dictionnaires Arabes*. 2 vols. Leiden: E. J. Brill, 1881.

Driver, G. R. "Studies in the Vocabulary of the Old Testament IV." *JTS* 33 (1932) 38–47.

________. "Notes on the Psalms." *JTS* 36 (1935) 147–56.

________. "Problems in Job." *AJSL* 52 (1935–36) 160–70.

________. "Supposed Arabisms in the Old Testament." *JBL* 55 (1936) 101–20.

________. "Linguistic and Textual Problems: Jeremiah." *JQR* 28 (1937–38) 97–129.

________. "Notes on the Psalms I. 1–72." *JTS* 43 (1942) 145–60.

________. "Hebrew Notes on 'Song of Songs' and 'Lamentations'." *Festschrift für Alfred Bertholet*. Ed. W. Baumgartner et al. Tübingen: J. C. B. Mohr, 1950, 134–46.

________. "Problems of the Hebrew Text and Language." *Alttestamentliche Studien*. Ed. H. Junker and J. Botterweck. Bonn: Peter Hanstein Verlag, 1950, 46–61.

________. "Problems in the Hebrew Text of Proverbs." *Bib* 32 (1951) 173–97.

________. "Ezechiel: Linguistic and Textual Evidence." *Bib* 35 (1954) 145–59; 299–309.

________. "Problems and Solutions." *VT* 4 (1954) 225–45.

________. "Birds in the Old Testament II. Birds in Life." *PEQ* 87 (1955) 129–40.

________. "'Another Little Drink' – Isaiah 28:1–22." *Words and Meanings: Essays Presented to David Winton Thomas*. Ed. P. Ackroyd and B. Lindars. Cambridge: University Press, 1968, 47–67.

________. "Isaiah I–XXXIX: Textual and Linguistic Problems." *JSS* 13 (1968) 36–57.

________. "Genesis XXXVI 24: Mules or Fishes." *VT* 25 (1975) 109–10.

Ellenbogen, M. *Foreign Words in the Old Testament*. London: Luzac, 1962.

Emerton, J. A. "The 'Mountain of God' in Psalm 68:19." *History and Traditions of Early Israel*. Ed. A. Lemaire and B. Otzen. Leiden: E. J. Brill, 1993, 24–37.

Finkelstein, L. ed. *Rab Saadia Gaon: Studies in His Honor*. New York: The Jewish Theological Seminary of America, 1944.

al-Firūzābādī. *Al-Qāmūs al-Muḥīṭ*. 4 vols. Beirut: al-Muʾassasa al-ʿArabīya lil-Ṭibāʿa wal-Našr, 1970.

Gätje, H. "Arabische Lexikographie." *Bustan* 5 (1964) 3–11.

Gluck, J. J. "Proverbs XXX 15a." *VT* 14 (1964) 367–70.

Grabbe, L. L. *Comparative Philology and the Text of Job: A Study in Methodology*. Missoula, MT: Scholars Press, 1977.

Greenstein, E. L. "Medieval Bible Commentaries." *Back to the Sources*. Ed. B. W. Holtz. New York: Summit Books, 1984, 213–59.

________. "YHWH's Lightning in Psalm 29:7." *Maarav* 8 (1992) 49–57.

Guillaume, A. "The Arabic Background of the Book of Job." *Promise and Fulfillment: Essays Presented to S. H. Hooke in Celebration of His Ninetieth Birthday*. Ed. F. F. Bruce. Edinbourgh: T. & T. Clark, 1963, 106–27.

________. *Hebrew and Arabic Lexicography*. Leiden: E. J. Brill, 1965.

Hava, J. G. *Arabic-English Dictionary*. Beirut: Catholic Press, 1951.

Haywood, J. *Arabic Lexicography*. Leiden: E. J. Brill, 1965.

Hirschberg, H. "Some Additional Arabic Etymologies in Old Testament Lexicography." *VT* 11 (1961) 373–85.

Hirschfeld, H. *Literary History of Hebrew Grammarians and Lexicographers*. Oxford: Oxford University Press, 1926.

Ibn Duraid. *Al-Jamhara fīl-Luḡa*. 2 vols. Hayderabad: Oriental Publications Bureau, 1926.

Ibn Fāris. *Maqāyīs al-Luḡa*. 6 vols. Cairo: al-Dār al-Islāmīya, 1990.

Ibn Manẓūr. *Lisān al-ʿArab*. 20 vols. Cairo: Dār al-Miṣrīya lil-Taʾlīf wal-Tarjama, 1966.

al-Jauharī. *Al-Ṣiḥāḥ*, 2 vols. Beirut: Dār al-Ḥaḍāra al-ʿArabīya, 1974.

Johnstone, W. "*YDʿ* II, 'Be Humbled, Humiliated'?" *VT* 41 (1991) 49–62.

Kamhi, D. J. "The Root *ḥlq* in the Bible." *VT* 23 (1973) 235–39.

Koehler, M. and W. Baumgartner. *Hebräisches und Aramäisches Lexicon zum Alten Testament*. 4 vols. Leiden: E. J. Brill, 1967–1990.

Kopf, L. "Arabische Etymologien und Parallelen zum Bibelwörterbuch." *VT* 8 (1958) 161–215.

________. "Arabische Etymologien und Parallelen zum Bibelwörterbuch." *VT* 9 (1959) 247–87.

Kraemer, J. "August Fischers Sammlungen zum Arabischen Lexicon." *ZDMG* 105 (1955) 81–105.

Krotkoff, G. "*Laḥm* 'Fleisch' und *leḥem* 'Brot'." *WZKM* 62 (1969) 76–82.

Lane, E. W. *Arabic-English Lexicon*. 8 vols. London, 1863–93; reprint, Beirut: Librairie du Liban, 1980.

Littauer, M. A. "The Figured Evidence for a Small Pony in the Ancient Near East." *Iraq* 33 (1971) 24–30.
MacIntosh, A. A. "A Consideration of Hebrew נער." *VT* 19 (1969) 469–79.
________. "The Meaning of *MKLYM* in Judges XVIII 7." *VT* 35 (1985) 68–77.
Margalit, B. "Ugaritic Contributions to Hebrew Lexicography." *ZAW* 99 (1987) 391–404.
Moscati, S. "The 'Aramean Ahlamu'." *JSS* 4 (1959) 303–7.
Moscati, S., A. Spitaler, E. Ullendorff, and W. von Soden. *An Introduction to the Comparative Grammar of the Semitic Languages*. Wiesbaden: Harrassowitz, 1964.
Müller, H.-P. "Die Wurzeln עיק, יעק, und עוק." *VT* 21 (1971) 556–64.
Nöldeke, T. *Die semitischen Sprachen: Eine Skizze*. Leipzig: T. O. Weigel, 1887.
North, F. S. "The Four Insatiables." *VT* 15 (1965) 281–82.
Pope, Marvin. *Job*. AB 15; Garden City, NY: Doubleday, 1965.
Reider, J. "Etymological Studies in Biblical Hebrew." *VT* 4 (1954) 276–95.
Renan, E. *Histoire Génerale et Système Comparé des Langues Sémitiques I*. Paris: Michel Lévy Frères, 1855.
Rosenthal, E. I. J. "Saadya Gaon: An Appreciation of His Biblical Exegesis." *BJRL* 27 (1942) 168–78.
________. "Saadya's Exegesis of the Book of Job." *Saadya Studies*. Ed. E. I. J. Rosenthal. Manchester: Manchester University Press, 1943.
________. "Medieval Jewish Exegesis: its Character and Significance." *JSS* 9 (1966), 265–81.
Rudolph, W. "Ein Beitrag zum hebräischen Lexikon aus dem Joelbuch." VTSup 16. *Hebräische Wortforschung*. FS W. Baumgartner. Leiden: E. J. Brill, 1967, 244–50.
______. *Joel – Amos – Obadja – Jona*. Gütersloh: Mohn, 1971.
Saiz, J. R. Busto. "בוראיך (Qoh. 12,1), reconsiderado." *Sef* 46 (1986) 85–87.
Sasson, Victor. "The Word *TRKB* in the Arad Ostracon." *VT* 30 (1980) 44–52.
Segert, S. "Hebrew Bible and Semitic Comparative Lexicography." VTSup 17. Leiden: E. J. Brill, 1968, 204–11.
Sezgin, F. *Geschichte des arabischen Schriftums VII*. Leiden: E. J. Brill, 1982.
Smith, J. Payne, ed. *A Compendious Syriac Dictionary*. Oxford: Clarendon, 1976.
Spitaler, A. "Arabisch." *Linguistica Semitica: Presente e Futuro*. Ed. G. Levi della Vida. Roma: Centro di Studi Semitici, 1961, 115–38.
Thomas, D. W. "Notes on Some Passages in the Book of Proverbs." *VT* 15 (1965) 271–79.

Ullendorff, E. "Comparative Semitics." *Linguistica Semitica: Presente e Futuro*. Ed. G. Levi della Vida, Roma: Centro de Studi Semitici, 1961, 13–32.

Wahrmund, A. *Handwörterbuch der neu-arabischen und deutschen Sprache*. 3 vols. Giessen: J. Ricker'sche Verlags-Buchhandlung, 1898.

Wechter, P. *Ibn Barūn's Arabic Works on Hebrew Grammar and Lexicography*. Philadelphia: Dropsie College, 1964.

________. "Ibn Barūn's Contribution to Comparative Hebrew Philology." *JAOS* 61 (1941) 172–187.

Wehr, Hans. *A Dictionary of Modern Written Arabic*. Ithaca: Spoken Language Services, 1976.

Wild, S. *Das Kitāb al-ᶜAin und die arabische Lexikographie*. Wiesbaden: Harrassowitz, 1965.

________. "Arabische Lexicographie." *Grundriß der arabischen Philologie 2*. Ed. H. Gätje. Wiesbaden: Harrassowitz, 1987, 37–47.

Wright, W. *Lectures on the Comparative Grammar of the Semitic Languages*. Cambridge: Cambridge University Press, 1890.

al-Zabīdī. *Tāj al-ᶜArūs*, 10 vols. Libya, n.d.

Zimmerman, F. "Problems and Solutions in the Book of Jonah." *Judaism* 40 (1991) 580–89.

Zimmern, H. *Vergleichende Grammatik der semitischen Sprachen*. Berlin: Reuther & Reichard, 1898.

Author Index

Scripture Index

Index of Arabic Forms

Index of Hebrew Forms

The Catholic Biblical Quarterly
Monograph Series (CBQMS)

1. Patrick W. Skehan, *Studies in Israelite Poetry and Wisdom* (CBQMS 1) $9.00 ($7.20 for CBA members) ISBN 0-915170-00-0 (LC 77-153511)
2. Aloysius M. Ambrozic, *The Hidden Kingdom: A Redactional-Critical Study of the References to the Kingdom of God in Mark's Gospel* (CBQMS 2) $9.00 ($7.20 for CBA members) ISBN 0-915170-01-9 (LC 72-89100)
3. Joseph Jensen, O.S.B., *The Use of tôrâ by Isaiah: His Debate with the Wisdom Tradition* (CBQMS 3) $3.00 ($2.40 for CBA members) ISBN 0-915170-02-7 (LC 73-83134)
4. George W. Coats, *From Canaan to Egypt: Structural and Theological Context for the Joseph Story* (CBQMS 4) $4.00 ($3.20 for CBA members) ISBN 0-915170-03-5 (LC 75-11382)
5. O. Lamar Cope, *Matthew: A Scribe Trained for the Kingdom of Heaven* (CBQMS 5) $4.50 ($3.60 for CBA members) ISBN 0-915170-04-3 (LC 75-36778)
6. Madeleine Boucher, *The Mysterious Parable: A Literary Study* (CBQMS 6) $2.50 ($2.00 for CBA members) ISBN 0-915170-05-1 (LC 76-51260)
7. Jay Braverman, Jerome's Commentary on Daniel: A Study of Comparative Jewish and Christian Interpretations of the Hebrew Bible (CBQMS 7) $4.00 ($3.20 for CBA members) ISBN 0-915170-06-X (LC 78-55726)
8. Maurya P. Horgan, *Pesharim: Qumran Interpretations of Biblical Books* (CBQMS 8) $6.00 ($4.80 for CBA members) ISBN 0-915170-07-8 (LC 78-12910)
9. Harold W. Attridge and Robert A. Oden, Jr., *Philo of Byblos,* The Phoenician History (CBQMS 9) $3.50 ($2.80 for CBA members) ISBN 0-915170-08-6 (LC 80-25781)
10. Paul J. Kobelski, *Melchizedek and Melchireš*[c] (CBQMS 10) $4.50 ($3.60 for CBA members) ISBN 0-915170-09-4 (LC 80-28379)
11. Homer Heater, *A Septuagint Translation Technique in the Book of Job* (CBQMS 11) $4.00 ($3.20 for CBA members) ISBN 0-915170-10-8 (LC 81-10085)
12. Robert Doran, *Temple Propaganda: The Purpose and Character of 2 Maccabees* (CBQMS 12) $4.50 ($3.60 for CBA members) ISBN 0-915170-11-6 (LC 81-10084)
13. James Thompson, *The Beginnings of Christian Philosophy: The Epistle to the Hebrews* (CBQMS 13) $5.50 ($4.50 for CBA members) ISBN 0-915170-12-4 (LC 81-12295)
14. Thomas H. Tobin, S.J., *The Creation of Man: Philo and the History of Interpretation* (CBQMS 14) $6.00 ($4.80 for CBA members) ISBN 0-915170-13-2 (LC 82-19891)
15. Carolyn Osiek, *Rich and Poor in the Shepherd of Hermes* (CBQMS 15) $6.00 ($4.80 for CBA members) ISBN 0-915170–14-0 (LC 83-7385)
16. James C. VanderKam, *Enoch and the Growth of an Apocalyptic Tradition* (CBQMS 16) $6.50 ($5.20 for CBA members) ISBN 0-915170-15-9 (LC 83-10134)

17. Antony F. Campbell, S.J., *Of Prophets and Kings: A Late Ninth-Century Document (1 Samuel 1-2 Kings 10)* (CBQMS 17) $7.50 ($6.00 for CBA members) ISBN 0-915170-16-7 (LC 85-12791)
18. John C. Endres, S.J., *Biblical Interpretation in the Book of Jubilees* (CBQMS 18) $8.50 ($6.80 for CBA members) ISBN 0-915170-17-5 (LC 86-6845)
19. Sharon Pace Jeansonne, *The Old Greek Translation of Daniel 7-12* (CBQMS 19) $5.00 ($4.00 for CBA members) ISBN 0-915170-18-3 (LC 87-15865)
20. Lloyd M. Barré, *The Rhetoric of Political Persuasion: The Narrative Artistry and Political Intentions of 2 Kings 9-11* (CBQMS 20) $5.00 ($4.00 for CBA members) ISBN 0-915170-19-1 (LC 87-15878)
21. John J. Clabeaux, *A Lost Edition of the Letters of Paul: A Reassessment of the Text of the Pauline Corpus Attested by Marcion* (CBQMS 21) $8.50 ($6.80 for CBA members) ISBN 0-915170-20-5 (LC 88-28511)
22. Craig Koester, *The Dwelling of God: The Tabernacle in the Old Testament, Intertestamental Jewish Literature, and the New Testament* (CBQMS 22) $9.00 ($7.20 for CBA members) ISBN 0-915170-21-3 (LC 89-9853)
23. William Michael Soll, *Psalm 119: Matrix, Form, and Setting* (CBQMS 23) $9.00 ($7.20 for CBA members) ISBN 0-915170-22-1 (LC 90-27610)
24. Richard J. Clifford and John J. Collins (eds.), *Creation in the Biblical Traditions* (CBQMS 24) $7.00 ($5.60 for CBA members) ISBN 0-915170-23-X (LC 92-20268)
25. John E. Course, *Speech and Response: A Rhetorical Analysis of the Introductions to the Speeches of the Book of Job, Chaps. 4-24* (CBQMS 25) $8.50 ($6.80 for CBA members) ISBN 0-915170-24-8 (LC 94-26566)
26. Richard J. Clifford, *Creation Accounts in the Ancient Near East and in the Bible* (CBQMS 26) $9.00 ($7.20 for CBA members) ISBN 0-915170-25-6 (LC 94-26565)
27. John Paul Heil, *Blood and Water: The Death and Resurrection of Jesus in John 18-21* (CBQMS 27) $9.00 ($7.20 for CBA members) ISBN 0-91570-26-4 (LC 95-10479)
28. John Kaltner, *The Use of Arabic in Biblical Hebrew Lexicography* (CBQMS 28) $7.50 ($6.00 for CBA members) ISBN 0-91570-27-2 (LC 95-45182)

Order from:

The Catholic Biblical Association of America
The Catholic University of America
Washington, D.C. 20064